# Tanks of World War II

by Duncan Crow

*Published by*

**PROFILE PUBLICATIONS LTD.**
**Windsor, Berkshire, England**

ISBN 85383 061 1


First published in 1979 by
PROFILE PUBLICATIONS LTD.

*Printed in England*
by R. J. Acford Ltd.

# CONTENTS

Coloured illustrations by Gordon Davies, Uwe Feist, Terry Hadler, and Michael Roffe.

# Acknowledgments

This book is based on the Profile AFV/Weapons series of which the author is the Editor. The numerous issues in the series which are relevant to FIGHTING TANKS OF WORLD WAR II were written by a number of internationally acclaimed experts in the field of armor and armored warfare. To them I give my thanks: Major J. K. W. Bingham, Royal Tank Regiment (retd.), J. M. Brereton, Peter Chamberlain, Hilary L. Doyle, Major-General N. W. Duncan, CBE, DSO, DL (retd), Chris Ellis, Christopher F. Foss, Lieutenant-General Tomio Hara, Imperial Japanese Army (retd), Colonel Robert J. Icks, Army of the United States (retd), John F. Milsom, Lieutenant-Colonel M. C. Norman, Royal Tank Regiment, R. M. Ogorkiewicz, W. J. Spielberger, and B. T. White.

    Photographs are via Colonel R. J. Icks, Imperial War Museum, E. C. Armées, General Hara, U.S. Army, R.A.C. Tank Museum, John Milsom, Chamberlain Collection, Dottore Nicola Pignato, Australian War Memorial, and the author's own collection.

                                   D.C.

NOTE

This book is not concerned with all armor. It is specifically concerned with tanks. It does not deal with armored cars or, except peripherally, with self-propelled guns and armored personnel carriers.

1 ton = 2,240 lbs.

*Panzer I Ausf. Bs entering Warsaw after it had been forced to capitulate on September 27, 1939.*

# I
# 1939: German Campaign Against Poland

World War II opened with the German attack on Poland on 1 September 1939. It was a short campaign lasting barely a month in which the Germans overwhelmed a valiant but poorly equipped army. The hammer-blows of the German invasion were delivered by their six Panzer and four Light divisions with overwhelming air support.

The first three of Germany's panzer, or armored, divisions were formed on 15 October 1935 — the 1st, commanded by General Freiherr von Weichs, at Weimar; the 2nd, under Colonel Heinz Guderian, at Würzburg; the 3rd, under General Fessman, in Berlin. Each division was a mixture of all arms — the key to German successes during the first half of the war. It had a panzer brigade, a motorized rifle brigade, an armored reconnaissance battalion, an anti-tank battalion, an artillery regiment, a signals battalion, and a light engineer company.

The first public appearance of a German panzer division — which was in fact an improved copy of the British Experimental Armoured Force of 1927/28 — was in 1937 during the autumn manoeuvers in Mecklenburg, when the show-piece was an attack by 800 tanks and 400 aircraft. The tanks by later World War II standards were little more than "sardine-tins" but in their massed array they were sufficiently impressive to give birth to the legend of the invincible panzers which, as much as the early actions themselves, gave Germany an important psychological edge throughout much of World War II.

For many years after the defeat of 1918 the German General Staff — and especially Heinz Guderian, that genius in the use of tanks who was, as he admitted himself, a disciple of the type of warfare propounded by the British armor experts Liddell Hart, Fuller, and Martel — had been debating three principles of tank fighting: the use of tanks in close co-operation with infantry; the independent use of tanks to break through and penetrate into the enemy's defensive positions; and the best use of air co-operation. In order to decide on the type of tank to be built and the type of formation in which tanks should be organized it was necessary to choose between one or other of the first two principles: one sacrificed speed, the other armor protection.

Guderian had no doubt which principle was the more important. In 1929 he had become convinced that "tanks working on their own or in conjunction with infantry could never achieve decisive importance." "My historical studies," he wrote in his memoirs, "the exercises carried out in England and our own experiences with mock-ups had persuaded me that tanks would never be able to produce their full effect until the other weapons on whose support they must inevitably rely were brought up to their standard of speed and of cross-country performance. In such a formation of all arms, the tanks must play the primary role, the other weapons being subordinated to the requirements of the armor. It would be wrong to include tanks in infantry divisions: what was needed were armored divisions which would include all the supporting arms needed to

1

*Panzer I Ausf. As moving through a battered street in Granadella during the Nationalist offensive in Catalonia towards the end of the Spanish Civil War*

allow the tanks to fight with full effect."

Guderian's view prevailed. The final decision favored speed, together with close support dive-bombing to give maximum striking power.

The tanks of the first panzer divisions were the Panzer I and Panzer II.

## Panzer I

The Panzer I was a light tank weighing 5.7 tons, mounting two 7.92mm machine-guns, and carrying a crew of two at a speed of 25mph with a maximum of 15mm armor. Its design had started in 1932 and was based on the British Vickers-Carden-Loyd light tanks. The first production models appeared in 1934 and were known as the PanzerKampfwagen I (PzKpfw or Pz I) Ausfuehrung A (Ausf A). The following year Ausf B entered production. The Ausf B had a Maybach-Krupp air-cooled engine that developed more power than the original air-cooled type of the IA. 500 of Ausf A and 2000 of Ausf B were built. The Ausf B was 14′6″ long, 6′9″ wide, and 5′7″ high.

The Panzer I was first tested in action in the Spanish Civil War where the inadequacies of a two-man crew and the lack of anti-tank armament were made abundantly manifest. A number of Panzer IIs also served with the Franco forces and both those and the Panzer Is gave valuable experience to the German army. Spain, indeed, provided the dress rehearsal for the *Blitzkrieg* against Poland and the West when, towards the end of the Civil War, motorized columns pushed forward 25 miles a day in the Aragon battle and even faster during the drive through Catalonia. Furthermore, the enormous influence of air superiority was clear to all who saw it.

More experience was gained from the moves into Austria and Czechoslovakia. Defects that were revealed in March 1938 during the Anschluss with Austria were remedied before the occupation of the Sudetenland later in the year. The occupation of the rest of Czechoslovakia, carried out 15 and 16 March 1939 in hard weather conditions showed that panzer divisions could operate on frozen roads and in difficult country. For example, one panzer division on the first day of the march to Prague covered nearly one hundred miles over bad roads in a snowstorm without a single vehicle being disabled.

## Panzer II

The Panzer II first appeared in 1935 as Ausf a1. This was followed by a2, a3, and b, each of which had successive improvements in engine cooling and suspension. These models all had a suspension system similar to that of the Panzer I: the front road wheel sprung independently on a coil spring and the remaining wheels in pairs on leaf springs linked by a girder. But the next model, Ausf c, had a different form of suspension with five medium-sized road wheels each independently sprung on leaf springs. Ausf c, like earlier Panzer II models and the Panzer I, had a rear-mounted engine with transmission through front driving sprockets.

Panzer II Ausf c weighed 8.7 tons with a 140 hp Maybach engine. It was 15′7″ long, and 7′0″ wide, and 6′6″ high. Its two vital improvements over the Pz I were that it had a three-man crew and a 2cm cannon as well as a machine-gun. The importance of this latter improvement was that the tank had an anti-tank capability; machine-guns could not penetrate even the minimum thickness of enemy armor. The importance of a three-man crew was that it improved the command situation because if the commander was also his own gunner — as he was in a two-man tank — he was obviously less able to spot his targets and direct his driver than a commander who was independent of these responsibilities.

The next models of the Panzer II were Ausf A, B, and C which appeared between 1937 and 1940. There was little difference between these models. The 1937 tanks, which marked the real start of mass production, showed little change from Ausf c. To improve protection the nose plate was changed and became angular and of welded construction instead of being round in shape and cast in construction. Gun mantlets were slightly changed with flanges at the top and bottom of the internal moving shield, presumably to avoid lead splash. Otherwise the turret was unchanged escept for a periscope in Ausf A and a cupola in B and in subsequent models to improve the commander's observation facilities.

The Panzer II Ausf D and E, of which 250 were produced in 1938 and 1939 were faster versions of the standard tank. Turret, superstructure, engine and transmission showed no difference from the earlier models, but the suspension was completely different. There were now four large wheels on each side, their movement controlled by torsion bars. Ausf D and E could reach 35 mph as compared with the 25 mph of earlier models. Their cross-country performance however was slower than the others. Because of disappointment with their performance the Ausf D and E were taken out of service and 95 were converted to flame-throwing tanks.

Panzers Is and Panzer IIs were 90 per cent of the total German tank force that invaded Poland - 2,886 out of 3,195.

## Light Divisions

By the 1 September 1939 when the Polish campaign began the Germans had six panzer divisions (1st, 2nd, 3rd, 4th, 5th, and 10th), plus the Panzer Lehr battalion, the Ordnance Department's own unit for testing and demonstration, which was equipped with Panzer IIIs and IVs. All took part in the campaign, the Panzer Lehr battalion and a Reconnaissance Demonstration battalion as part of Guderian's XIX Army Corps at his special request. Although the Panzers III and IV had short-barrelled guns and thus indifferent anti-tank performances, for tank penetration demands high velocity and high velocity increases with the length of the barrel, nonetheless within a

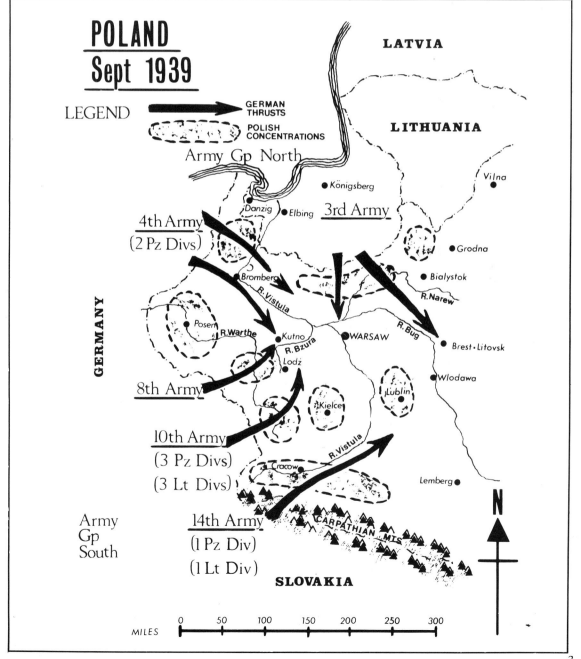

POLAND
Sept 1939

LEGEND

GERMAN THRUSTS

POLISH CONCENTRATIONS

LATVIA

LITHUANIA

Army Gp North

Königsberg

Vilna

Danzig

Elbing

3rd Army

Grodna

4th Army
(2 Pz Divs)

Bromberg

R. Vistula

Bialystok

R. Narew

GERMANY

Posen

R. Warthe

Kutno

R. Bzura

WARSAW

R. Bug

Brest·Litovsk

8th Army

Lodz

Wlodawa

10th Army
(3 Pz Divs)
(3 Lt Divs)

Kielce

Lublin

Cracow

R. Vistula

Lemberg

N

Army Gp South

14th Army
(1 Pz Div)
(1 Lt Div)

CARPATHIAN MTS

SLOVAKIA

0    50    100    150    200    250    300

MILES

matter of days after the Polish campaign had ended the Panzers III and IV were accepted as standard equipment for all tank battalions on Hitler's orders and, as we shall see during the course of this book, were to be the tanks that took the panzer divisions across Europe from the Atlantic to the Volga and along the North African littoral from Tripoli to El Alamein.

In addition to these six panzer divisions there were, as already mentioned, four light divisions which together made the cutting edge of the German invasion of Poland. These light divisions were the German cavalry's counterwork to the panzer divisions. Just as the cavalry in Great Britain strongly resisted any loss of identity or surrrender of ground to the Royal Tank Corps, so the German cavalry subtly opposed the encroachment of the Panzers. The German cavalry, the proud Uhlans and their colleagues, reacted just as the Lancers, Hussars, and Dragoon Guards of the British army reacted. Tanks! Ugh!! But tanks were the future, and the horse for all its arch-necked pomp was long ago in the past as World War I had shown.

To play the panzers at their own game the German cavalry formed light divisions, each of which had two motorized rifle regiments of two battalions each, a reconnaissance regiment, an artillery regiment, and a lorry-borne light tank battalion, as well as supporting units.

## Polish Tanks

The panzer and light divisions, backed by division after division of infantry that is the solid core of all armies, 44 divisions in all, fell upon Poland and destroyed it with armor and dive-bombers. To counter this the Poles had little to offer except courage. The majority of Polish armor was the TK3 and TKS tankettes, "sardine-tins", closely modelled on the British

Carden-Loyd Mark VI Light Armored Vehicle which they built under license. The TKS had a four-cylinder Polish built Fiat engine instead of the four-cylinder Ford Model A engine in the TK3 and the Carden-Loyd. The armor was up to a maximum of 8mm in the TK3 and 10mm in the TKS. In both the armament was a single 7.92mm machine-gun mounted in the front right hand side of the hull.

The Poles also had horsed cavalry in profusion and they were about to produce a 10TP Medium tank which was a Polish version of the Christie M1931 Medium of which we shall hear more for it proved to be one of the seminal tanks in the history of armor.

## "Six-Ton" Tank

One other tank the Poles had. It too was derived from another seminal tank - the Vickers-Armstrongs "Six-Ton" tank which was produced in 1929 as a private venture. During the next ten years the tank was sold to Bolivia, Bulgaria, China, Estonia, Finland, Greece, Japan, Portugal, Romania, Russia, and Siam (Thailand), as well as to Poland. It influenced tank design in many countries being either copied or built under license. One machine which was acquired for a 30-day trial by the United States Army contributed several of its features to a new American light tank the T2 which was the progenitor of the M2-M5 series, the Stuarts.

There were two types of the "Six-Ton" tank: Type A which had a crew of three and was armed with two Vickers machine-guns each mounted in a separate turret, the turrets being placed side by side; and Type B which had a single turret with a short 47mm gun and a co-axial machine-gun. The duties of the three-man crew were commander, gunner, and driver. The Type B appeared in 1930.

*Panzer I Ausf. A showing twin MGS in turret.*

*Vickers Six-Ton Tank Type B with a single turret mounting a 47mm gun and coaxial machine-gun.*

Both Type A and Type B were powered by an Armstrong-Siddeley eight cylinder 90 hp air-cooled engine, which gave a maximum road speed of 22 mph (cross-country 15 mph). The engine was situated at the rear of the tank with the transmission led forward to drive front sprockets. Steering was of the clutch and brake type. Type A with a 13mm armor basis weighed 7.2 tons, Type B with a 17mm basis weighed 7.4 tons.

The remarkable feature of the Type B was that it gave the same main turret armament and armor protection as the Medium Mark III which Vickers were at the time producing for the British Army, at a fraction of the Mark III's cost and weight. Furthermore its mechanical reliability was high and it set new standards in track life with a manganese steel skeleton type track.

## 7TP Light Tank

In Poland the Six-Ton tank was built as the 7TP. It appeared at first in both Type A and Type B versions but later production models, incorporating improvements, were built only in the Type B version. In a special Polish turret, built in Sweden, was a 37mm Bofors and a coaxial machine-gun. The 7TP weighed 9.5 tons, had an armor basis of 25mm and a maximum of 40mm, and was powered by a 110hp diesel engine. Its maximum speed was the same as that of the Six-Ton tank. Its suspension, too, was the same - two pairs of twin bogies on rocker with leaf springing. It was 15' long, 7'11" wide, and 7'2" high.

In addition to the tanks bought from Vickers the Poles built about 170 7TPs and these were the backbone of their armored force. Though numerically much weaker than the TK3 and TKS tankettes which totalled some 700 there was no comparison as far as firepower was concerned. In fact the 7TPs were better than the Panzers I and II which were the bulk of the German armor. But althoug their range of 100 miles was comparable with the panzers' 90 their power to weight ratio was greatly inferior. The power-weight equation is vital to the evaluation of a tank as a vehicle for it reveals, irrespective of the weight of the tank or the size of its engine, the degree of efficiency reached in balancing these two vital factors. The power-weight ratio of the 7TP was 10 horse power per ton, compared with the Panzer Is 24.6 and the Panzer IIs 16.1.

## Panzer 35 (t)

After the Polish campaign the four German light divisions were converted to panzer divisions — the 6th,

*Panzer II Ausf. D and E being loaded on to transporters. Note large Christie-type suspension wheels.*

7th, 8th, and 9th. The 6th, 7th and 8th were equipped with Czech tanks which had been taken over by the Germans when they over-ran Czechoslovakia in March 1939. Each of these divisions had only one panzer regiment of three battalions as opposed to the earlier divisions with their two panzer regiments each of two mixed tank battalions. The 9th, which was equipped with German tanks, had one panzer regiment of two battalions.

The Germans took over two types of Czech tank, the LT-35 and the LT-38 which they re-designated respectively the Panzer 35(t) and the Panzer 38(t), the (t) being an abbreviation of (tscheche), the German for Czech. Both were light tanks.

The Pz 35(t) was a 10.5 ton tank with a crew of four — commander, gunner, loader/wireless operator, and driver. It was 15'1½" long, 7'0½" wide and 7'4½" high, and was armed with a Skoda 37mm L/40 gun and two 7.92mm Besa machine-guns, one of them coaxial, the other in the hull front fired by the driver. Armor thickness ranged from 12mm on the floor to 35mm on the hull nose and turret mantlet. In order to leave the fighting compartment as free as possible from all power train elements, the tank had rear sprocket drive from the engine which was a 6-cylinder water-cooled in-line OHV Skoda T-11 of 120hp at 1,800rpm which gave a maximum speed of 25mph. The power-weight ratio was only 11.4 and the range was 120 miles.

The suspension of the Pz 35(t) was eight small bogie wheels each side, coupled in pairs and mounted on the hull in fours on a rocker arm with inverted semi-elliptic leaf springs. There was a small guide wheel between the front idler and the first bogie wheel, and there were four return rollers each side. The durability of the suspension was remarkable in that track and bogie wheel life was from 4,000 to 8,000 kms.

The vehicle was easy to drive thanks to its 12-speed gearbox and pneumatic-servo-mechanical steering unit, and trips of 125 miles in a day could be achieved at average speeds of 12-16mph.

*Panzer II Ausf. A which started to appear in 1937. The improved suspension, seen here, was first used on the previous model, Ausf. c.*

With the annexation of Czecho-Slovakia the Germans took over 106 LT-35s which were in due course issued to the 6th Panzer Division. By June 1942, when Czech tank production had been suspended, the number of Pz 35(t)s in Wehrmacht service had increased to 167. The Hungarians produced an extensively modified version of the LT-35 called the Turan II and Hungarian units equipped with these fought alongside the Wehrmacht in Russia..

## Panzer 38 (t)

The LT-38 had its origins in 1933 when the Czech firm CKD began to design a light tank series for export. The series had a factory designation LT (Lehky Tank - Light Tank) L. The first model was LTL-H, also called, by the Czech Defence Ministry, the TNHB, and for export purposes the LT-34. By 1938 the series had developed to a model called the TNHS (LTL-P) which had improved armament and armor.

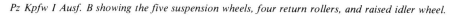

*Pz Kpfw I Ausf. B showing the five suspension wheels, four return rollers, and raised idler wheel.*

After tests it was chosen, with alterations, as the standard tank for the army and 150 were ordered. It was designated TNHP or LT-38. CKD exported 196 of the series to a number of countries including Sweden, Switzerland, Peru, Latvia, Yugoslavia, and Afghanistan. One was bought by Great Britain for evaluation purposes.

The TNHP weighed 8 tons and was armed with a 37mm (Model Skoda A7) L/47.8 gun and a coaxial 7.92mm Besa machine-gun which could take independent action when required by means of its spherical mounting. A second 7.92mm Besa was mounted in the hull front - fired by the driver. There was a crew of four: commander, gunner, loader/operator, and driver. The dimensions were 14'9½" long, 6'9½" wide, and 6'9½" high. Armor thickness was 25mm on the front 19mm on the sides, and 15mm on the rear. The engine was a 6-cylinder water-cooled in-line Praga TNHP OHV developing 125hp at 2,200rpm and was mounted vertically on the centre-line of the vehicle in the rear compartment. Maximum speed was 35 mph and range was 125 miles. The power-weight ratio was a good 15.6. Drive was via front sprockets.

The suspension was four rubber-tired wheels each side, each mounted on a cranked stub-axle and each pair of wheels being controlled by a semi-elliptic spring freely pivoted. There were two return rollers each side.

Soon after they had taken over the Czech tank factories the Germans increased the armor thickness of the TNHPs under construction. Frontal armor became 50mm thick, and that on the sides 30mm. In some vehicles the German 37mm KwK L/45 gun was sub-

*Czech tank LT-35 (seen here in Russia) was issued to 6th Panzer Division as Panzer 35 (t).*

stituted for the original Czech one. The new model was called the TNHP-S (S standing for *schwer*, heavy), its weight increasing to 8.5 tons. The Germans had nine models of this tank, Ausf. A to F, S, G and H. The 90 tanks of Ausf. S had been built for the Swedish army and were impounded by the Wehrmacht. Ausf. H had a 150hp (at 2,600 rpm) 6-cylinder Model epa/AC Model IV engine and its weight was 9.7 tons.

A total of 1,168 Panzer 38(t)s were built for the Germans, and even when production of gun-tanks ceased

*PzKpfw 35 (t) in German unit service.*

*Fourth production model TNHP (Ausf D) in German service as Panzer 38(t).*

early in 1942 because the 38(t) was by then out-classed the chassis continued to be produced for various German self-propelled guns until the end of the war.

The Pz 38(t) took part in the Polish campaign and then saw service in Belgium, France, Yugoslavia, Greece, and Russia. There were 228 in the 7th and 8th Panzer Divisions for the May-June campaign in 1940 and by July 1941 the number in service had risen to 763. Indeed during 1940-41 the Panzer 38(t) formed a quarter of the German tank force.

*Eighth production model TNHP (Ausf G). Two panzer divisions, the 7th and 8th, were equipped with Panzer 38(t)s.*

*Panzer IV, Ausf. C, at St. Martin de Fresnay, France.*

# II
# 1940: German Campaign in the West

Late in the evening of 9 May 1940 a vast murmur of men and hum of engines could be heard by outposts facing the Germans from the Dutch frontier to Luxembourg. It was an awesome sound that puzzled its hearers. Within hours its meaning was clear. At 0400 hours on the 10th *Sichelschnitt,* the code name for the attack on the west began. German parachutists landed in Holland and Belgium and ground forces crossed the Dutch, Belgian, and Luxembourg frontiers. In the van were the panzer divisions. It was they, with their dive-bomber support, which brought about the fall of France.

For his attack on France Hitler had 136 divisions on the Western Front. These included ten panzer divisions and the SS Panzer Regiment "Liebstandarte Adolf Hitler". Between them they had some 2,500 tanks. Guderian was still commanding XIX Corps and still had the Armored Reconnaissance Demonstration battalion under command! The numbers of different types of tank were: Panzer I 500, Panzer II 955, Panzer III 349, Panzer IV 278, Panzer 35(t) 106, Panzer 38(t) 228 - Total 2,416. Although the Panzer IIs were the most numerous the core of the attack was provided by the Panzer IIIs which proved to be a decisive factor in this brilliantly conducted campaign.

In most accounts of German armor in World War II the two tanks which tend to feature largest are the Panther and the Tiger, possibly because of their charismatic names which give them more of a "personality" than the tanks that were known simply by numbers. But important as those two tanks were when they appeared on the battlefield later in the war, their importance - taking the war as a whole — was far less than that of the Panzer III and Panzer IV. These were the two tanks, first the Panzer III and then after 1942 the Panzer IV, that made the reputation of the German armored forces. In terms of production alone their importance is made clear:

| | | |
|---|---|---|
| Panzer III | 5,644 | (12 Ausführungen) |
| Panzer IV | 9,000 | (9 Ausführungen) |
| Panther | 4,814 | (4 Ausführungen) |
| Tiger Ausf E | 1,350 | |
| Koenigstiger | 484 | |

Both tanks owed their inception to Guderian. The Panzer III was to be the new Panzer army's standard vehicle, with the Panzer IV as its heavier-gunned support. The Panzer III was designed by Daimler-Benz, the Panzer IV by Krupp, both being chosen from a number of competitors.

*On April 9, 1940 Germany invaded Denmark and Norway. A Panzer I Ausf. A is seen here on the road to Kolding in Jutland, Denmark, on April 11.*

*Panzer I in southern Norway, April 1940. Norwegian resistance did not end until June 9.*

## Panzer III

The chassis design of the Panzer III reflected the influence of the automotive industry since it featured independent suspension and, as finally developed, torsion bar springs. Krupp, by contrast, in the design which it had also submitted, with its long experience of locomotive construction favored the more traditional leafsprings and bogie wheel mountings.

Ten vehicles were made of the first production model, Ausf. A, eight of them mounting a 37mm gun. Ausf. A, in common with other early models in the series, was intended for development purposes and its suspension consisted of five large road wheels supported by coil springs. Front sprocket drive and rear idler wheels, together with two return rollers, completed the running gear. Weight was 15.1 tons, armor was 5 to 14.5mm thick. A Maybach HL 108 TR 12-cylinder gasoline engine gave it a top speed of 20 mph. The basic hull, turret, and superstructure remained unchanged throughout the Panzer III's production life. There was a five man crew: commander, gunner, loader, driver, radio operator.

The hull consisted of three separate sub-assemblies — the main hull, the front superstructure carrying the turret, and the rear superstructure covering the engine compartment. All these units were of single skin welded construction and the individual assemblies were bolted together. The hull section was divided into two compartments by means of a bulkhead, the front one housing the gearbox and steering mechanism. The front plate of the superstructure supported the ball-mounted machine-gun which was manned by the radio operator. Hinged escape doors were centrally placed on both sides of the hull, though these were eliminated from the last two models. The top front plate of the main hull had hinged doors, giving access to the brake mechanism and providing means of escape for the crew.

The welded turret had no rotating platform, but the commander and the gunner had their seats suspended from the turret and thus traversed with it. There were large hinged double doors on the turret sides. As well as the main armament, which in the earlier models was a 37mm and in the later a 50mm gun, there was a co-axial 7.92mm machine gun mounted in the turret. Models up to later Ausf E had two machine-guns.

The second model in the series, Ausf B, appeared in 1937. The only basic change was in the suspension. There were now eight bogie wheels per side, two bogies each supported by one large horizontal leafspring. The number of return rollers was increased to three — an identifying feature for all Panzer IIIs thereafter. Ausf B, C, and D all had the eight-wheeled suspension system, only the spring arrangement differed. Armor thickness on the Ausf B and C was still 14.5mm. Fifteen of each were produced. On the Ausf D the armor was increased to 30mm bringing the total weight to 21 tons. As well as the slight variation in the leafsprings the other change in the Ausf D was that it had a six-speed ZF transmission instead of the previous five-speed gearbox. Thirty Ausf D were built.

The next model, Ausf E, was the last of the development models. Built from 1939 to 1940 this vehicle had a new engine (Maybach HL 120 TR) with an output of 300 hp compared with the 230-250 hp of the earlier models, and a new transmission (Maybach Variorex), as well as a major change in the suspension system which now had transverse torsion bars with independent road wheels. Forty-one Ausf E were produced.

When Guderian had first envisaged the Panzer III he had wanted it to be armed with a 5cm gun. The Ord-

*Panzer II Ausf. A. Note horn-type periscope on turret top (centrally behind guns) which distinguishes Ausf. A from subsequent models; also absence of cupola. Background suggests tank is passing through Flemish square.*

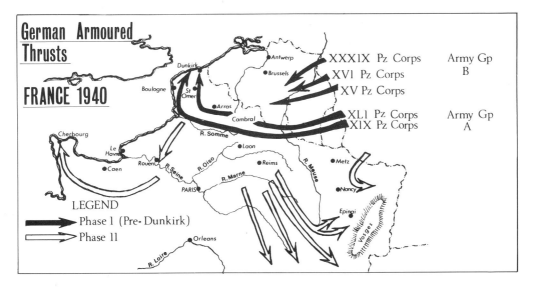

German Armoured Thrusts

FRANCE 1940

XXXIX Pz Corps
XVI Pz Corps    Army Gp B
XV Pz Corps

XLI Pz Corps    Army Gp A
XIX Pz Corps

LEGEND
→ Phase I (Pre- Dunkirk)
⇒ Phase II

nance Department settled for a 37mm gun because this was the weapon that had been issued to the infantry as their anti-tank gun and the benefits of standardization outweighed other considerations. But by 1938 the Ordnance Department had themselves realised their error. They now authorised development of an up-gunned version. Krupp were asked to develop the turret to mount a 5cm gun, the turret ring diameter having been made big enough even in the earliest models to accommodate this without basic changes. The new gun mount, however, was not ready by the time the first major production version of the Panzer III, the Ausf F, appeared in early 1940, so this tank too had a 37mm gun, as did early production Ausf G. Ausf F had a modified version of the Maybach power plant. Ausf E was 17'8" long, 9'7" wide, 8'0" high.

## Panzer IV

While it was the Panzer III that provided the core of the attack against the West in 1940, spearheaded the attack against Russia in 1941, and carried the main load of the battles in the Middle East from February 1941 to May 1943, in the long run it was its "stable companion", the Panzer IV, which proved to be the most durable of German tanks. Its first prototype appeared in 1936, in 1945 it was still in production - the only German tank which remained in production and troop service throughout World War II, a fact which demonstrates its sound basic design and the brilliant foresight shown in its conception.

In laying down the prerequisites for armored fighting vehicles in 1933-34 Guderian had specified their order of priority: mobility, fire-power, armor protection, and communication. A five-man crew was also considered essential. In his *Profile* of the Panzer IV Walter Spielberger wrote that the distinct allocation of duties between the crew which this number allowed gave German tanks their marked tactical superiority over their Allied counterparts despite other shortcomings. "Guderian's insistence on supplying the crews with communication systems, usable not only between tanks but also on intercom, was another key factor enabling these vehicles to be used as practical and

effective units of the newly-created armored force, trained in the disciplined and co-ordinated art of armored warfare. However, despite these major advantages, most German tanks of the development period could not be considered superior in Guderian's first three requirements of mobility, fire-power and armour protection. In fact many of the French tanks opposing the German attack of 1940 had heavier armour, while the British cruisers were superior in manoeuvrability. What the Allied armour lacked most, " in Spielberger's opinion, "was the administrative backing of supply and maintenance required by modern mechanized forces, and the fighting efficiency afforded by well-designed crew compartments."

Because the Panzer IV was only to be a support vehicle for the new Panzer army's standard tank the Panzer III, production for the first few years was on a limited scale. The first model, Ausf A appeared in 1936. There were 35 of them. The following year 42 Ausf B were built. In 1938 Ausf A was seen in public for the first time, and Ausf C and D came off the production line. These four models were the Panzer IVs that took part in the Polish campaign. In December 1939 production of Ausf E began and the first 20 of Ausf F left the factory in February 1940.

Krupp's first proposals for the suspension of the Panzer IV were for interleaved road wheels of the type that was later adopted for the Panther and the Tiger. *Panzer III Ausf E in France, May 1940.*

*Panzer IV Ausf. A of 1st Panzer Division, only 35 of this model were built. Ausf. A had stepped front plate with driver' position protruding at left, round bow machine-gun mount at the right. Driver had single centre vision slit and rectangular side view opening in front plate.*

*Panzer 38(t) commander's tank – Panzerbefehlswagen 38(t).*

But the form actually adopted was much simpler and was used throughout the whole life of the tank. Eight smallish road wheels each side were suspended in pairs on leaf springs, with the idler wheel off the ground at the rear end and the top run of the track carried on four return rollers. Just as the three return rollers were a recognition feature for the Panzer III so were the four for the Panzer IV.

The engine, situated at the rear, was the 12-cylinder Maybach HL 108 TR in the Ausf A, the larger HL 120 in the Ausf B and first Ausf C vehicles, and the HL 120 TR M (as in Panzer III Ausf F) from then on. The weight of Ausf A was 17.3 tons, of Ausf B 17.7

tons, of Ausf C 20 tons, and by Ausf E it had gone up to 21 tons giving a power to weight ratio of 14.3 Range on roads was 125 miles.

The armor basis for the hull of Ausf A was 14.5mm and 20mm for the turret. In Ausf B- E the frontal armor was increased to 30mm, and then to 50mm in Ausf F. The main armament in all these models was the short-barrelled 7.5cm KwK L/24 with HE capability. There was a coaxial 7.92mm machine-gun and all except Ausf B and C also had another machine-gun in the hull front to the right of the driver. The Ausf B was 19'3" long, 9'4" wide, 8'6" high.

*Ausf. E of 13th Panzer Division early in the Russian campaign, 1941. This model still had the stepped front plate, although with modification to the driver's visor and the bow machine-gun mount. Other changes included: modified commander's cupola installed further forward so that it no longer protruded from the back plate of the turret which was now unbroken; increased armor on nose plate, bolted on armor for hull to improve fighting compartment protection (see picture), spaced armor in front of bow machine-gun and sometimes in front of driver's position; replacement of rectangular ventilator flap on turret roof by fan ventilator, and removal of cone-shaped single port flap which was replaced by a flat lid (see picture: the new ventilator is half-way along the turret roof in front of the cupola).*

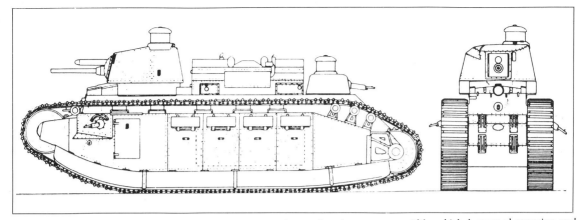

*These drawings of the Char 2C show the proportions of great length to narrow width, which hampered steeering and maneuverability.*

## Allied Tank Strength

On 10 May 1940 the French army had 94 divisions on the North-East front. Of these 70 were infantry, three armored, three light mechanized, five cavalry (partly mechanized), and 13 garrison equivalents. The British Expeditionary Force had 10 divisions in the line, all infantry. One under-strength armored division (the 1st) started to cross to France the week after *Sichelschnitt* began — its move had been arrranged some time before — and there were two battalions of an independent tank brigade, as well as a number of mechanized cavalry regiments for reconnaissance. The Belgian army had 22 divisions.

Unlike the Poles, the French and their allies, especially the French, had plenty with which to counter the German attack. The legend grew up after 1940 that the German tanks greatly outnumbered the allied tanks and that that was why they were so successful in their scythe sweep which made a panzer corridor from the Meuse to the Channel and then, when the northern armies had been cut off and destroyed in May, turned south and west in *Fall Rot* (Operation Red) to complete the destruction of France. This was not so. The French had 3,438 modern tanks of which 2,283 were on the North-East front. As well as those in the armored and mechanized formations there were 1,123 in independent tank battalions whose role was infantry support. And, to complete the roll, there were 534 World War I Renault FTs engaged on airfield protection and tasks of that nature. These old Renault light tanks were not included in the total of 3,438.

Apart from numerical parity, if not superiority, much of the Allied tank strength was as good or better than the German. The French Char B and S35 were considerably better protected than any tank the Germans had as were the British Matildas.

## French Tank Development

In France as in the United States the tank after World War I was officially decreed to be an infantry weapon,

*Char 2C had a crew of 13 and weighed 68 tons. This one was captured by the Germans on its way to the front.*

to be developed by and for the infantry. In consequence two types of tank were thought to be needed: a heavy "breakthrough" tank (*char de rupture*) and a light versatile battle tank (*char de bataille*), the latter to replace the Renault FT of which 3,767 were still in service in 1921. By 1926 the Renault NC as a replacement for the FT had reached an advanced stage of development, but the idea of an all-purpose light tank was found to be impractical and the NC was not adopted by the French Army. Some were sold to the Japanese, however, who did not find them at all satisfactory.

The *Programme de 1926* defined the need for three classes of tank: a light tank of less than 13 tons for close support of infantry; a battle tank of between 19 and 22 tons to be used in conjunction with the light tanks and for taking on heavier resistance as well as enemy tanks; and a heavy tank of up to 70 tons for supporting infantry and the lighter tanks

In the light tank class a new Renault D appeared in 1931 weighing 12 tons, in the battle tank class was the Char B weighing 25 tons, the first prototype of which appeared in 1929, and in the third class was the Char 2C, a 68 ton tank with a crew of 13 already in service since 1921 but few in number.

After manoeuvres in 1933 the classifications were changed yet again. The light tank was to be a "6-ton" tank, the battle tank was to be a medium with both the Char B and the Renault D being put in this category, and the heavy tank was still the Char 2C.

Meanwhile, in 1931, ideas were developed for forming an armored force for the cavalry role completely separate from the tanks of the infantry. Three classes of armored vehicle would be needed and they were defined as: *auto-mitrailleuse de découverte* (AMD) for long-range reconnaissance; *auto-mitrailleuse de reconnaissance* (AMR) for local reconnaissance; and *auto-*

*mitrailleuse de combat* (AMC) capable of supporting the other two classes in engaging enemy armoured vehicles. Specifications for all three were issued. The AMDs developed were all armoured cars. The AMRs were built by Renault — first the 33VM based on experience with the NC, then the 35 ZT. In 1940 there were 384 AMRs in service. The AMC specifications resulted first in the Renault 34 YR which was the first French light tank to carry a 3-man crew, and then in a modified version with new suspension, a longer track, and a more powerful engine, known as the AMC Renault ACG 1. The specification was then changed.

Although the cavalry were now developing tracked vehicles the legal distinction between theirs and the infantry's — as in the United States. The *Direction de la Cavalerie* developed wheeled and tracked *autos-mitrailleuses*, literally machine-gun cars, while the *Direction de l'Infanterie* developed *chars*. Nevertheless while their basic concepts on the employment of armour were quite different the requirements of both arms gradually merged into producing similar vehicles. For instance, the Chars Hotchkiss H35 and H39 which were designed to meet the infantry specification for a light tank were rejected by the infantry in favour of a similar Renault tank (the R35) and were forthwith adopted by the cavalry, only to be accepted by the infantry at a later stage to the extent that in the long run in 1939/40 the infantry were deploying as many Chars Hotchkiss as the cavalry and using them in exactly the same role as the R35.

## R35 and H35

The R35 was the new light tank, the "6-ton" tank, called for after the 1933 manoeuvres. In fact it weighed 10 tons, had a crew of two, was armed with a 37mm gun

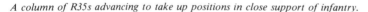

*A column of R35s advancing to take up positions in close support of infantry.*

*H39. The driver sat on the right side of the tank compared with the R35 where he sat on the left.*

and a machine-gun, had maximum armor of 40mm, a speed of 12.5mph and a range of 90 miles. The R35 became the most numerous light infantry tank in service in 1940; more than 1,600 were built.

The hull of the R35 was in three cast sections which were bolted together with rolled armor plates that made up the sides and floor. A cast armor front section housed the differential and final drive assembly, while the rear section included two access doors to the engine at the back end and carried the idler wheels (tensioners). The two side plates carried the suspension assemblies and front driving sprocket. The suspension was similar to that of the other Renault light tanks of the cavalry, with five wheels each side, one mounted independently and two pairs on bell-cranks in a "scissors" arrangement acting upon each other through rubber springs between the upper arms. Three top rollers carried the

track forward and the trailing idler wheel, mounted low, may have helped to improve stability.

The driver sat on the left, while the engine and transmission were on the right. In the Hotchkiss tanks the reverse was the case. The commander stood on the floor of the fighting compartment, but was supported by a seat which was suspended from and rotated with the turret. Access to this position was by a door at the back of the turret. A fire-proof partition separated the fighting compartment from the rear part, which included the Renault 4-cylinder 82hp engine, with radiator and fuel supply. Brake bands in the differential, operated by the steering levers, controlled the drive through epicyclic gears to each track in a simple but effective regenerative system that reduced loss of power when steering. This Cletrac system (known as such after the commercial tractor built by The Cleveland Tractor Company in the

15

later 1930s) was used in the other French light tanks and also in American light and medium tanks.

Stemming as it did from the same requirement as that for the R35, the Hotchkiss H35 had similarities with the Renault tank. Both had the APX turret of cast armor with the 37mm gun and 7.5mm machine-gun, both had a two-man crew, both in fact looked very much alike. But as well as the position of the driver (left in the Renault, right in the Hotchkiss) there was another quick recognition point of difference between them: the suspension. The H35 had six wheels on each side mounted on bell-cranks arranged in pairs as opposed to the R35's two and a half "scissors".

There was no turret floor in the H35 and the commander/gunner sat on a saddle which was suspended from and moved with the turret. The engine was a 6-cylinder Hotchkiss 75hp giving a speed of 17.5mph. The range was 80 miles. The infantry rejected the tank because it was reported that the suspension gave poor cross-country mobility and that it was under-powered. The cavalry was not convinced by these reports, and in view of the infantry's later change of opinion it was probably right. The H35 weighed 11.4 tons, was 14'1" long, 6'0" wide, and 7'1" high.

Both the R35 and H35 had successors in the R40 and the H39. The latter was a more powerful version of the H35 with a 120hp engine, which gave the tank an almost horizontal engine deck compared with the downward sloping deck of the H35. Some H39s had the short L/21 37mm gun with a muzzle velocity of 1,273 ft/sec, as in the H35, but others had the long L/33 37mm gun with a

muzzle velocity of 2,300 ft/sec. Over 1,000 Hotchkiss tanks were built.

The R40, some of which also had the L/33 37mm gun, was developed by AMX (Moulineaux Arsenal) with a new suspension that gave a better cross-country performance. It consisted of 12 small wheels each side mounted in pairs with vertical coil springs, the whole protected by skirting plates. Two battalions were equipped with R40s in 1940.

## Chars D1 and D2

Until the R35 arrived under the pressure of rearmament in 1936 the only new tanks that had been issued to the infantry since the first World War were the Chars D, also built by Renault, and a few Chars B.

The Char D1 retained the same form of one-man turret carried on a high, vertical-sided superstructure as the NC and had the same type of suspension. The 65hp engine was slightly more powerful than that of the NC, and the tank was appreciably larger to give more room for the three-man crew and for wireless equipment. Its dimensions were 18'7" long, 7'2" wide, 7'7" high and it weighed 12 tons. Maximum armor was still only 30mm, but there was better all-round protection and skirting plates were added over the suspension. Armament on the first tanks consisted of a 47mm gun in the turret, with a fixed machine-gun in the hull fired by the driver. An improved version had a co-axial machine-gun as well as the hull gun, armor up to 35mm and a 100hp engine. Most of these were used in North Africa.

The Char D2 was an improved version of the D1,

*Waiting is a necessary part of war. R35 and its crew.*

*Compared with the H39, a point of recognition at the rear of the R35 is the prominent exhaust pipe leading to the silencer on the left track guard.*

with the same armament but with heavier armor so that its battle weight was 20 tons. In appearance, however, the tanks were appreciably different, the D2 having the Puteaux cast APX 1 turret which was also mounted on the Char B1, stowage bins on the track guards, and mud chutes below the top track rollers. With 40mm of armor the D2 was fairly well protected, but it had a design weakness in that it offered an almost vertical front hull face.

## Char B

The Char B prototype of 1929 had a crew of four, a maximum of 25mm armor, and, in line with the thinking of the period that a tank's main purpose was "man-killing", was armed with four machine-guns — two in the hull front and two coaxially in the one-man turret — as well as a 75mm gun in a hull mounting beside the driver. The engine was a 6-cylinder Renault of 180hp which gave the tank a top speed of 17.5mph. It had a radius of action of 10 to 12 hours. Prototype trials continued. By 1935 the armor had increased to 40mm and weight to 28 tons. Although its advanced technical merits had confirmed the Char B1, as it was now called, as a powerful weapon there was a drawback in the complexity of its components which meant that it was costly to build and that it was unsuitable for short service conscripts to operate and maintain. A complicated tank is all right for regular soldiers who have ample time to learn and understand its ways, but sophistication can be a hindrance in a conscript army. That was one of the reasons why the American Sherman was so valuable — it was a "straightforward" tank.

The German re-occupation of the Rhineland in March 1935 was a warning for the future. Rearmament became the watchword. In April the decision was taken to build 40 Char B1, up-armored to 60mm, and to be called the Char B1 *bis*. The extra armor added four tons

to the weight and to cope with it the engine was boosted to 300hp, but at the expense of a reduced radius of action. In the course of development the number of machine-guns had been reduced and a cast APX 1 turret carrying a 47mm gun and one machine-gun was installed. For the B1 *bis* the turret was changed to the similar but thicker APX 4 with a better high velocity 47mm gun. The Char B1 *bis* became the principal French medium tank with 365 plus 35 Chars B1 built before the defeat of France in 1940.

The Char B1 *bis* was 21' 5" long, 8' 3" wide, 9' 2" high. Its hull was formed by cast armor components bolted together with armored plates resting on two cross members and on girders along each side. The suspension assemblies, which incorporated vertically mounted coil springs, were fixed to these girders so that the springs projected upwards into the hull; skirting plates protected the suspension system below. The hull

*H39s in German service. These tanks mount a searchlight above the gun and the cupola has been changed to one with flat top and hatches.*

17

*Although fairly well armored (40mm) the Char D2 offered an almost vertical front hull face.*

was divided by a fireproof bulkhead into two parts, with the fighting compartment at the front holding the crew of four (commander, driver/gunner, loader, radio operator), and the engine and transmission at the rear.

"The driver, who was a key member of this crew in that he also fired the main weapon, sat on the left front; and he was the only one apart from the commander who had the means to see what was happening outside," wrote Major Bingham in his *Profile* of the tank. "Fixed to a shield on his right was the elevating handwheel for the 75mm gun that was mounted behind a mantlet bolted to the hull front on the right. However, the gun was fixed in azimuth, and laying for line was effected by swinging the tank. An unusual feature for a tank gun was the air-blast gear fitted to the 75mm gun and supplied from a Luchard air compressor. Fumes from the gun were literally blown out through the muzzle in a way that is standard in naval gun turrets.

*Char B1 bis under test 1940.*

"The driver was also, often, responsible for firing (by cable) the fixed machine-gun that was mounted low in the hull to the right of the 75mm gun, although, by repositioning the firing handle to the tank roof, this could be done by the tank commander. There was limited movement of the machine-gun in elevation by a turn-buckle on the mounting but, like the 75mm gun, it was fixed for line."

The driver was a key member indeed!

But the loader too was a busy man. In action he had to serve both hull guns as well as replenishing the ammunition for the commander's gun in the turret — and serving the 75 meant fitting the fuses, stowed separately. The radio operator and the loader were seated at the base of the commander's seat. The commander was the sole occupant of the turret which was towards the rear of the fighting compartment.

"The gearbox and transmission unit incorporated a differential connected directly to the final drive and sprockets, together with an auxiliary differential controlled by the Naeder hydrostatic system for steering. In conjunction with this double differential unit, the Naeder system controlled power distribution to each track and permitted the infinitely fine variations in steering which were vital in aiming the gun. Brake drums were mounted externally at each end of the auxiliary differential, operated with servo-assistance by the driver's hand brakes and pedal. If necessary these brakes could be used for steering."

The suspension was a development of the Holt tractor type. There were three main assemblies each side, each of four bogies mounted in pairs on plates pivoted at the centre; each of these plates was mounted at the end of a similar one balanced at the base of the vertically mounted coil springs that projected upwards into the hull, while semi-elliptic leaf springs also came into play as dampers under extreme compression. In addition, but not bearing the weight of the tank, there were four independently mounted bogies (three forward, one rear) controlled by leaf springs. Unusually, the front idler wheel (tensioner) was also spring-mounted, and adjustments for track tension were made from inside the fighting compartment.

"All in all," wrote Major Bingham, "the Char B was a sophisticated tank with some technically advance features, but its very complexity was a disadvantage in manufacture and maintenance, while its layout and demands on the crew hindered an efficient use of its weapons in battle ... It was regarded as a very powerful weapon in its day."

Two other medium tanks deserve a brief mention. The Char B1 *ter*, of which only five were built, was an improved version of the B1 *bis*, giving the 75mm hull gun a limited traverse and carrying an extra crewman who was described as a mechanic. The AMX 38 was a 1.6 ton tank with 60mm of armor and a 47mm gun. It had a 150hp Aster diesel engine but its radius of action was only 90 miles and with a crew of two its use in battle would have been limited. In fact it was never used in combat. Only a few were built.

## FCM 36

As well as the R35 another light infantry tank resulted from the "6-ton tank" specification and was accepted

*The driver' position in the Char B1 bis with gun elevating handwheel and firing gear on his right. Note the compressed air pipe to the air blast gear on the gun for expelling fumes.*

*Left side of the SOMUA S35, showing the crew's access door below the turret and other hatches for access to the engine compartment. The cupola has the domed roof.*

for service by the infantry, unlike the Hotchkiss H35. This was the FCM 36 (FCM — Forges et Chantiers de la Méditerranée). In prototype form it weighed 10 tons without crew and ammunition. It had a 90hp Berliet diesel engine, Type MDP, which gave it a speed of 15mph and a range of 140 miles. It carried an APX turret with the same armament as the R35 — 37mm gun and coaxial machine-gun. In its final form it had an unusual octagonal turret rising to a fixed commander's cupola, but carried the same guns. The hull and skirts over the suspension were made up of angled, sharply sloping plates which offered a mosaic of surfaces to increase ballistic protection. The suspension was of the same type as that of the Char B1, mounted *à poutre*, with two assemblies of four bogie wheels in pairs on each side, controlled by vertical coil springs, and single wheels independently at the front. In action this suspension revealed a weakness against damage by mines, nor did the mosaic of welded armor plates stand up well to attack. Two battalions were equipped with the 100 FCM 36 that were built. The tank was 14′ 8″ long, 7′ wide, 7′ 8″ high, and had a two-man crew.

## Divisions Légères Mécaniques

The idea of an armored force for the cavalry role bore fruit in the permanent formation in 1934 of the *Ire Division Légère Mécanique*. This was one year before the first panzer division was formed and four before the first British armored division. However the DLM was not the result of new thoughts on armored warfare as the British Experimental Mechanized Force had been in 1927. On the contrary it had evolved in the process of cavalry mechanisation, which was just as unpopular among the French *dragons* and *cuirassiers* as it was among the Uhlans and the British hussars, and although its organisation resembled that of the panzer division its role was limited to the performance of traditional cavalry tasks.

A second DLM was formed in 1938, a third in August 1939, and a fourth was being assembled in May 1940 but was never completed.

The DLM consisted of a combat brigade of two armored regiments each of 87 tanks (including reserves), a reconnaissance regiment with two squadrons of armored cars and two of motor cyclists, and a motor-ized rifle regiment with three battalions of *dragons portés* — that each included a squadron of tracked *autos-mitrailleuses*. One of the armored regiments was equipped with light tanks, the H35/H39, the other with medium tanks.

The cavalry's medium tank, built to the new specification that was issued in 1934, was the Char 1935-S, more commonly known in English as the S35. The fact that the S35 was called a *char de cavalerie* destroyed the dishonest pretence that the cavalry used only *auto-mitrailleuses* and not tanks.

## S35 Tank

The S35 was developed from the D1 and D2 and was designed and built by SOMUA (*Société d'Outillage Mécanique et d'Usinage d'Artillerie*). It was powerfully armed for the time with a 47mm L/34 gun (muzzle velocity 2,200 ft/sec) and a coaxial 7.5mm Reibel machine-gun so mounted as to give limited independent traverse. It carried thick armor — 56mm on the turret sides, 40mm on the hull front and sides. And it showed a remarkable speed (25mph) for its weight of 19.5 tons. It had a 190hp Somua V8 engine and a range of 160 miles.

The hull design was ingenious and represented a notable advance in the use of cast armor. There were

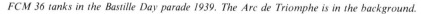

*FCM 36 tanks in the Bastille Day parade 1939. The Arc de Triomphe is in the background.*

three sections bolted together. The lower part, stretching the full length of the tank, was an open container for the engine, transmission and controls, to the sides of which the suspension assemblies were bolted. The other two parts formed the superstructure which covered the top of the container and was bolted to its rim, the rear part covering the engine and transmission, the front part enclosing the fighting compartment and carrying the turret. The joint between the lower part and the superstructure was a weakness in the tank because an anti-tank missile hitting it on this joint would split the hull open.

There were no partitions in the fighting compartment so that the three-man crew were not separated from each other. The driver sat on the left, the radio operator on the right. There were two radio sets. The commander, who was also the gunner, sat on a saddle which rotated round a post bolted to the floor. The APX 4 turret was the same as that on the Char B1 *bis* and the D2. Steering was by a double differential system that was similar to but simpler than the hydrostatic unit fitted in the Char B and as such was much more advanced than the Cletrac.

The suspension system was on the same principle as the Panzer 35(t) which was also used on the Italian M11/39. On each side were two assemblies of four bogie wheels mounted in pairs on articulated arms controlled by semi-elliptic leaf springs. A ninth bogie wheel at the rear was fitted independently with a coil spring. The wheels were of steel, with rims rising to a centre flange that ran in a groove in the centre of the track plate and so guided the movement of the track since there were no horns on the track plates to prevent the track from sliding off sideways. Two return rollers with similar flanges and two skids with guiding keys on

*Captured S35s with German crews driving in line ahead through the Arc de Triomphe in Paris after June 1940.*

top carried the track forward to the tensioner wheel at the front. The lower part of the assemblies was protected by armor plate.

### French Armored Division

As well as the four DLMs the French had two other types of armored formation — the *Division Légère de Cavalerie* and the *Division Cuirassée de Réserve*. The DLC was a smaller and weaker version of the DLM, apart, that is, from the DLC's horsed brigade. As well as this it had a mechanized brigade with a combat group of light tanks, a reconnaissance group of armored cars, and two battalions of *dragons portés*. There were five DLCs. The DCR was a more formidable affair. It had two *demi-brigades* each of one battalion of 33 Chars B and one of 45 H39s, together with one battalion of

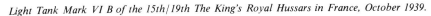

*Light Tank Mark VI B of the 15th/19th The King's Royal Hussars in France, October 1939.*

*Light Tanks Mark VI B of the 1st Royal Tank Regiment, 7th Armoured Division in the Libyan Desert. Cruisers in the background.*

motorized riflemen and supporting artillery and engineers. But it had neither air support, nor anti-aircraft defence, nor any means of reconnaissance. Nor did it have logistic support of its own for mobile operations. Its task, unlike that of the panzer division or the armored division, was confined to acting as a break-in force ahead of the infantry. The first DCR was formed in September 1939, the second in January 1940, and the third in March, while a fourth under General de Gaulle was put together haphazardly after the German attack had begun.

Although, in general, the French tanks lacked speed, a fact that inhibited tactical flexibility, it is true to say that they had a number of material advantages. But these advantages were lost. As Brigadier H. B. C. Watkins has written in his study of the panzer divisions, *Only Movement Brings Victory*, the reasons for this loss were "lack of an up-to-date tactical concept, lack of communications and so the lack of the ability to react with any flexibility to the enemy threat – defeat in detail was inevitable against tacticians of the class they had to face."

## British Light Tanks

By the time the Polish campaign was over the British had landed a small armored contingent as part of the British Expeditionary Force in France. Six of the infantry divisions had a reconnaissance regiment of mechanized cavalry equipped with tracked armored carriers and Mark VI Light tanks. These regiments were eventually removed from their role as divisional troops

*Policing the Empire – Light Tank Mark IIB Indian pattern on the North-West frontier of India.*

and formed into two recce brigades. There was also an armored car regiment for long range reconnaissance and a tank battalion (later increased to two) for close support of infantry. The under-strength 1st Armoured Division arrived in May 1940.

The Mark VI Light tanks were the culmination of a line of armored vehicle development that started in the 1920s with the one- and two-man tankettes built by Martel and the firm of Carden-Loyd. The Carden-Loyd light armored vehicles Marks I to VI led to the first Vickers light tank after Carden-Loyd had been taken over by Vickers in 1928. The Vickers Light Tank Mark I appeared in 1930, having evolved from the Carden-Loyd Mark VII prototype light tank, the first to have a traversing turret. The Mark I was followed by the Mark II (1930) which was the pattern on which all subsequent light tanks up to the Mark VI were based.

A second design path also came from the early Carden-Loyds. This was the lightly armored tracked machine-gun carrier without a turret which, unlike the light tank, was not intended for use as a fighting vehicle but was to be a means of transporting crew and fire power which were dismounted for action. Originally the weapon was a Vickers medium machine-gun but this was later replaced by a Bren light machine-gun — hence the title "Bren carrier". Two other specialized versions of the carrier — the Cavalry and the Scout — were produced, to be followed in 1940 by a Universal carrier which was suitable for all purposes, any special requirements being met by minor modifications. Bren and Scout carriers, despite the intention for which they were designed, frequently had to be used as close contact fighting vehicles during the 1940 campaign in France. The Universal carrier later became the most ubiquitous tracked vehicle in the British and Commonwealth armies.

The Mark VI Light tank had three variants — the VIA, VIB, and the VIC. Of these four tanks the VIB was by far the most numerous. It weighed 5.2 tons, was 13′ 2″ long, 6′ 10″ wide, and 7′ 5″ high. Its armament was two machine-guns, a 0.5 inch and a 0.303 inch, as was that of the Mark VI itself and the VIA. The VIC on the other hand had one 7.92mm Besa machine-gun and one 15mm Besa. The engine for all four was a Meadows 6-cylinder 88hp which gave a maximum speed of 35mph. It was in the right-hand side of the hull with the transmission led forward to drive front sprockets. Each of the four Mark VIs had a three-man crew, the Mark V being the first British light tank to have a third crew member. The driver sat on the left-hand side. The suspension consisted of two two-wheeled bogie units each side, sprung on inclined twin coil springs, the rear road wheel also acting as a trailing idler. The maximum armor thickness was only 15mm, the same as the German Panzer I.

Mark VIs had one very nasty habit. If you tried to steer it down a hill on the engine overrun you experienced an unpleasant phenomenon known as "reverse steering". Once the drive to one of the tracks had been disengaged by the steering clutch, the weight of the tank swung the free track round towards the one still engaged with the result that the tank went the opposite way to that intended. To guard against this you had always to steer with the engine pulling.

Apart from this and their doubtful value as fighting machines the Mark VIs were reliable, easily maintained, and fast. They were the backbone of the British armored forces at the outbreak of World War II and remained so for the next year. In September 1939 there were some 1,000 in service. In the next ten months 320 more were produced, mostly VIBs and some VICs. When the 1st Armoured Division went to France in May 1940 almost half its armor was still light tanks despite the substantial increase in the production of heavier tanks in the previous nine months. Nonetheless their lack of gun power and their inadequate armor for the duties they were called upon to fulfil both in France and in the Western Desert made them death traps and no one was sorry to see the back of them in the Desert in 1941. After Dunkirk the British General Staff lost interest in light tanks, preferring armored cars for the reconnaissance role. Light tank development passed to the United States and it was the American Stuart that replaced the Mark VIs in 1941.

The Mark VI and its variants were not the end of light tank development in Great Britain however. Although the British light tank was obsolescent as a type when they were produced from 1941 onwards there was also a Mark VII, the Tetrarch, and a Mark VIII, the Harry Hopkins. The Tetrarch is historic for two reasons: it was the first and last British airborne tank to see service, being used in the Madagascar landing in May 1942 and by the 6th Airborne Reconnaissance Regiment of 6th

*The first British tank, a Mark VIB, crosses to the Franco-Belgian frontier near Menin on 10 May 1940, the day the German attack on the West began.*

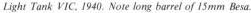

*Light Tank VIC, 1940. Note long barrel of 15mm Besa.*

*The suspension of the A.M.C. Renault 35 ACG 1 was similar to that of the Renault R35, but with five top rollers. Note the monocular periscope in the turret roof.*

*Panzer II Ausf F, which was up-armored on turret. The visor beside the driver's face visor (under the 20mm gun) was a dummy, presumably to confuse enemy anti-tank gunners. Conical idler wheel was a feature of Ausf F.*

*Three-quarter front view of Panzerspähwagen II (or Pz Kpfw IIL) – Luchs (Lynx) showing interleaved suspension wheels.*

*A Panzer III Ausf. F or G with the Afrika Korps in late 1941. It has the early cupola but re-spaced return rollers, plus the short 5cm gun.*

*A10s (Cruiser Mark II) in the Libyan Desert*

British Airborne Division in the Normandy landing in June 1944. Some were also sent to Russia with other British tanks in 1942. It was also the tank on which the DD Duplex Drive amphibious device was first successfully tested.

## British Tank Policy

To understand why there was such a preponderance of light tanks in the British armored force at the outbreak of war it is necessary to look briefly at what happened after 1918. Two factors determined the types and numbers of armored fighting vehicles produced in Britain during most of the years between 1918 and 1939: the first was the scenario about the army's role; the second was the small amount of money allotted for defense and within that meagre total the miniscule amount appropriated to armored vehicles.

As to the first factor the priorities of the army's role were considered to be: first, the policing of the British

Empire; second, minor expeditions and guerrilla warfare; third, major expeditions; and fourth — an unlikely contingency it was felt — a major war, and by that was meant a European war. Combined with the second factor this order of priorities resulted, as far as tanks were concerned, in vehicles that were small and, in military terms, inexpensive. Hence the light tank.

Not that strategic thinking was faithfully reflected in the incidence of tank production for in fact no one in authority seemed able to make up his mind exactly what the tank was supposed to do in the post-1918 army. Tanks were both disliked and feared by the older arms. Of crucial importance for the future was that the climate of opinion against tanks caused not only their design and supply to dwindle but it destroyed the soil for future growth as well. For years Vickers-Armstrongs were the only firm which was interested in tanks, and apart from them only the Royal Ordnance Factory at Woolwich did any work in this field.

In 1936, before rearmament began in earnest, the British army had 375 tanks, of which 209 were light tanks and the remainder mediums. Of these 375 all but 71 were officially classed as obsolete — the "moderns" being two Medium IIIs, 22 Mark V Lights, and 47 Mark VI Lights. During the three years that elapsed before the outbreak of war in September 1939 as well as several hundred more Mark VI Lights, the first of the new cruiser and infantry tanks that were to replace the old mediums were produced.

The two classes of cruiser and infantry, or I, tanks were the outcome of the conflict of views about a tank's purpose — whether it was purely an infantry support weapon, or whether its prime purpose was in mobile operations as the successor to the horsed cavalry.

*Cruiser Mark IVA – the up-armored A13 mounting a coaxial Besa 7.92mm machine-gun (A13 Mark IIA). The bracket on the side of the turret carried two dischargers which projected a 4-inch smoke canister about 150 yards. The A13 was the first British tank to have Christie suspension.*

*A column of A13s (Cruiser Mark IV) moving up in the Western Desert.*

## British Cruisers

The pilot model of the first of the new tanks, the A9 Cruiser Mark I, appeared in April 1936 and the first deliveries were made in January 1939. Also in 1936 the pilot A10 Cruiser Mark II appeared, but the first delivery was not made until December 1939. The A13 Cruiser Mark III had a speedier development period. The order for two pilots was given at the end of 1936 and two years later, December 1938, the first deliveries of the production series were made. By the beginning of September 1939, 79 cruisers (Marks I and III) had been produced and 77 were in service.

Both the A9 (Cruiser Mark I) and the A10 (Cruiser Mark II) were interim tanks that only went into limited production. The A9 was 19′ 3″ long, 8′ 4″ wide, and 8′ 4″ high and had a crew of six; 125 were built, including a number of close support tanks with a 3.7 inch mortar as the main armament instead of a 2 pounder gun. As well as a coaxial .303 inch Vickers machine-gun the A9 had two forward sub-turrets each with a Vickers

.303 mg. These sub-turrets were unpopular with crews. The tank had 14mm maximum armor thickness and weighed 12 tons. Its AEC 6-cylinder 150hp engine, similar to that used on buses, gave it a maximum speed of 25mph.

Production of the A10 was 170, including a number of Cruiser Mark IIAs which had a 7.92mm Besa coaxial instead of a Vickers, and another Besa in the hull front. This was the first British tank to mount a Besa. There was also a close support version of the A10. The A10 was 18′ 1″ long, 8′ 3½″ wide, and 8′ 6″ high. Its engine was the same as that of the A9 but the maximum armor thickness was 30mm and the tank weighed 13.75 tons so that in consequence the maximum speed was only 16mph. The A10 had a crew of five.

Originally the A10 was supposed to be an infantry support tank. Then it was re-designated as a "heavy cruiser". This classification was part of the pre-war canon that proliferated the designations and characteristics of armored fighting vehicles to make a variety in

*7th Panzer Division halted during its sweep across northern France to Cherbourg in June 1940. The division at this time was commanded by General Erwin Rommel. The tank on the extreme left is a Panzer 38(t).*

*Panzers I and II being prepared for embarkation. Apparatus for discharging smoke is fitted at tail. Note divisional sign on right-hand mudguard of right-hand tank and on tool chest of left-hand tank.*

which each closely defined type was intended to perform a closely defined role — a utopian ideal which would not have survived the confusion of battle. The A13 (Cruiser Mark III) was looked upon as a "light cruiser" because its maximum armor thickness was only 14mm. It weighed 14 tons, was powered by a Liberty V-12 340hp engine which gave it a speed of 30mph, had a crew of four, and was armed with a 2 pounder and a coaxial Vickers .303 inch machine-gun. It was 19′9″ long, 8′ 4″ wide, and 8′ 6″ high.

Because it was only a "light cruiser" it was assumed that the A13 would need the support in action of a "heavy cruiser". The A10 being only an interim type, three other heavy cruisers were embarked upon but none went beyond the prototype stage. The third of these projects was the A16 which was built in 1938 by Nuffield Mechanisations and Aero Ltd, a newly created armaments firm that built the A13 in 1937. The A13 was the first British tank to have Christie suspension and the A16 was a development of it. The Chief Superintendent of Design at Woolwich and Thompson Taylor co-operated with Nuffields in the building of the single A16 which was the first tank to have Dr H. E. Merritt's double differential steering mechanism. Used in conjunction with a Maybach propulsion gearbox this was called the Merritt-Maybach transmission. It was superseded in general use in British tanks by the Merritt-Brown transmission which had Merritt's later-developed triple differential system.

The specification for the "heavy cruiser" had called for a 2 pounder as the main armament, two forward hull machine-gun sub-turrets, 30mm of armor, a cross-country speed of 25mph, and a weight of 25 tons. While the A16 and A14 (which was the other "heavy cruiser" project to reach the prototype stage — the third project was cancelled at the design stage) were being built a second mark of A13 was produced with 30mm of armor which increased the tank's weight to 14.75 tons. Nevertheless it could still do 30mph. There appeared to be no advantage in the A14 and A16 over the up-arm-

ored A13, even though the latter did not have the forward hull sub-turrets, so both prototypes were cancelled.

The up-armored A13 (A13 Mark II) with hollow V sides added to the original A13 type turret was Cruiser Mark IV. It was 19′ 9″ long, 8′ 4″ wide, and 8′ 6″ high. The Mark IVA had a Besa instead of a Vickers coaxial machine-gun. Total production of A13 Marks I and II was 665.

Cruisers Marks I to IVA saw action in France in 1940 with the 1st Armoured Division and in the Western Desert in 1940 and 1941 with the 7th Armoured Division. The A9s and A10s left the battlefield on the Egyptian frontier during Operation Battleaxe in June 1941; the A13s, which still formed half the strength of 7th Armoured Brigade for Operation Crusader in November 1941, went after the fighting at Sidi Rezegh during that Operation.

"In my own experience," wrote Major James Bingham of the Royal Tank Regiment who fought in A13s in France and in A10s and A13s in the Desert, "these cruisers were, in their time and in the balance of gun-power and armour, the equal in quality with their German opponents — the Panzer III and Panzer IV. The weakness in France lay in numbers, when two armoured brigades of 1st Armoured Division with a total of about 150 hastily issued A9s and A13s landed at Calais and Cherbourg in May in an attempt to check the German *Blitzkrieg*. At Calais all were lost but some of the cruisers and light tanks south of the Somme returned to England after a series of long and tiring moves that ended in a grim race for Cherbourg against Rommel's 7th Panzer Division."

## More Panzer Divisions

After their victory in the west the Germans doubled the number of their panzer divisions. But there were as yet insufficient tanks to equip all the divisions to the original scale, so that the doubling was only nominal. Each tank brigade was reduced to one regiment. Six divisions each had a three-battalion regiment, but the remainder had only two battalions. The battalions, however, were more powerful. Each had two light companies equipped with up-gunned Panzer IIIs and one medium company with 75mm Panzer IVs. The infantry brigade now had two two-battalion motorized rifle regiments and one motor-cycle battalion. Anti-aircraft artillery became a regiment equipped with 88mm guns.

Production of Panzer IIs, IIIs, and IVs continued with the introduction of new models. For Operation Sea Lion, the planned invasion of England, a battalion of Panzer IIs was specially prepared with amphibious equipment that enabled them to float and be propelled. Three other battalions of amphibious tanks were also formed, consisting of Panzer IIIs and IVs which were made submersible. Sea Lion never materialized, and the amphibious tanks were used by 18th Panzer Regiment of 18th Panzer Division to cross the River Bug at the opening of the Russian campaign in June 1941.

## Up-Armored Panzer IIs

During 1940 the hollow charge anti-tank missile became a menace to be reckoned with and, with Hitler's agreement, it was decided that all German tanks would in future be up-armored by the addition of spaced plates to reduce the effect of these missiles. As far as the Panzer II was concerned this resulted in the Ausf F (Ausf G and J had minimal differences from F), which had 35mm of armor in the front and 20mm on the sides. Apart from that it looked exactly like Ausf C with engine, transmission, armament and suspension unchanged. Top speed, naturally, was reduced, but this had been an accepted disadvantage when up-armoring was authorised and was off-set by the hope of reducing the heavy crew losses that had occurred.

The final Panzer II was the Ausf L, called the *Luchs* (Lynx), which was the outcome of a specification given to Daimler-Benz in 1938 to design a new Panzer II with the principal emphasis on increased speed. The tank that eventually emerged in 1942 was an amalgam of that and the designs for two other tanks. The *Luchs*, intended primarily for reconnaissance, weighed 11.8 tons and was powered by a Maybach HL 66P 6-cylinder engine of 180hp. Maximum speed was 38mph. The suspension was five large overlapping wheels with torsion bar springing each side. There were no return rollers. This type of suspension ultimately led to the Panther and Tiger suspension in which overlapping became interleaving in order to reduce ground pressure, a step which brought its own problem in the shape of track jamming. The *Luchs* had a four-man crew. Its main armament on the first 100 vehicles was a 20mm gun, on the subsequent 35 it was a 50mm L/60 gun. All had a coaxial machine-gun. It was 15' 5" long, 8'3" wide, and 7' 1" high. Frontal armor was 30mm and the side plates 20mm.

As in the case of all other German tanks except the Panzer 35 (t), Panzer II chassis were used for self-propelled weapons. The production of Panzer II tanks ceased in 1942. Models D and E were converted top flame-throwers.

## Up-Gunned Panzer IIIs

Starting late in 1940 Panzer III Ausf E, F, and early G tanks were all converted to take the 5cm KwK L/42, al-

though this was against Hitler's own determination that they should be fitted with the longer and more powerful L/60 5cm gun. At the very end of 1940 the Ausf H appeared. This introduced a major change in the suspension system. The track width was increased, new final drive and idler wheels were used and the spacing of the return rollers was increased to give better support to the heavier track. A demand for thicker armor was met by adding 30mm plates to the front faces of both hull and superstructure. Ausf H remained in production for the early part of 1941. Some vehicles were later re-fitted with Hitler's choice — the L/60 gun. This was also the main armament of all but the first batch of the next model, Ausf J, which differed from its predecessors in having its basic armor increased from 30mm to 50mm. The Ausf J was built throughout 1941.

The next model, Ausf L, was externally almost identical to Ausf J, but there was the addition of a torsion bar compensator in the suspension to balance the nose-heaviness induced by the 5cm gun and the extra weight of the "spaced armor". Coiled springs were found to be insufficient to counteract the added weight. Weight of the tank was now 22.3 tons. The final two models of the Panzer III, Ausf M and N, appeared in 1942 — Ausf M with the hull escape door openings eliminated, Ausf N with the short L/24 75mm gun from the Panzer IV as its main armament. Panzer III production ceased in August 1943 and its production capacity given over to the self-propelled weapon with the same chassis, the Sturmgeschütz III (Stug III).

The Panzer III was a highly important tank in the history of armor development. Both it and the Panzer IV showed how a basic chassis could be progressively up-gunned, up-armored, and used for special purpose variants.

## Attack on the Balkans

In April 1941 Hitler invaded Jugoslavia and Greece. Five panzer divisions were involved in the attack on Jugoslavia (5th, 8th, 9th, 11th, and 14th) with one (16th) in reserve; two went into Greece (the 2nd and the 5th after Jugoslavia). Two months earlier two other panzer divisions under Rommel had been committed to the battle in North Africa where the British had been overwhelming the Italians. These two were the 15th and the 5th Light later re-designated 21st Panzer. Both were on the reduced establishment of two tank battalions and three motorized rifle battalions.

*Panzer III Ausf H in Sofia, 1941.*

*British light tanks in the Western Desert, 1940. They formed the bulk of the British tank strength at that time and bore the brunt of many desert actions. A Mark VIB is in the foreground.*

# III

# 1940-43: War in North Africa

The first shots in the Desert war were fired on 12 June 1940, two nights after Italy came into World War II on Germany's side. Reconnaissance elements of the British 7th Armoured Division cut their way through the wire that marked the frontier between Egypt and Italy's colonial province of Cyrenaica. The first phase ended with the defeat of the Italians at Beda Fomm in February 1941. The second phase began almost immediately, that same month, with the entry of Rommel and his Afrika Korps, and for the next eighteen months the action swung back and forth across the desert until the Germans and Italians had pressed the Eighth Army back to El Alamein some 60 miles from Alexandria. With the second battle of Alamein at the end of October 1942 the last phase began. Rommel was forced to retreat along the North African littoral towards Tunisia where fighting had been going on since the time of Alamein when Allied forces had landed in Morocco and Algeria. In May 1943 the Desert war ended near Tunis with the surrender of the German and Italian forces.

## Italian Armored Divisions

Three armored divisions were in the Italian army that fought in North Africa — the Centauro, the Littorio, and the Ariete. The Italian armored division was a combination of all arms as in most other armies. Each had an armored regiment of three medium tank battalions, an anti-aircraft company equipped with 20mm Breda

guns, and one *officina* or repair and recovery company. Each battalion had 50 tanks, 90 trucks, and 600 men. The division also had a bersaglieri (light infantry) regiment and an artillery regiment as well as engineers. Both the Ariete and Centauro divisions were formed early in 1939 from the 1st and 2nd Armored Brigades which had themselves been formed in 1937 as the Italian army reflected in its own organization the trends of thought about the use of armor that influenced armies in the 1930s. And in keeping with these trends the Italians also introduced light tanks into their cavalry, or fast, divisions, and had tank units allotted to infantry corps. Their main problem was lack of adequate equipment to carry out these various tasks. Right up to the 1939 manoeuvers they were still using Fiat 3000s, an Italian version of the French Renault FT, as one of their two tracked armored vehicles. The other was the CV L3.

## L3 Series

The Carro Veloce L3 (L = Light, 3 = 3 tons) originated in the British Carden-Loyd Mark VI. In 1929 twenty-five of these machine-gun carriers were bought by the Italian army and based on the Mark VI design a fast tank (carro veloce) was built by Fiat and Ansaldo. Designated the CV28 this was followed by improved models, the CV29, the CV L3/33 (33 = 1933), the CV L3/33II, and finally the CV L3/35. The L3/35 was powered by a

30

4-cylinder 43hp Fiat engine mounted transversely at the rear with a circular type radiator behind it. Transmission was led forward with final drive to front sprockets. Suspension was two three-wheel bogie units and a single unsprung road wheel each side. Each bogie unit was sprung on a quarter elliptic leaf spring. The top run of the track was supported on acacia wood rails. The fighting compartment was in the centre with the two crew-members — driver on the right, commander/gunner on the left — sitting almost side by side. Maximum armor was 13.5mm, armament was twin 8mm Breda 88 machine-guns. Despite its original description as a carro veloce the top speed of the L3/35 was only 26mph. Later the designation was changed to carro armato. Weight was 3.2 tons, length 10′4″, width 4′7″, height 4′2″. There was a flamethrower version of the L3/35 in which the flame projector replaced one of the machine-guns.

The L/33 was first used in action in December 1934 against Ethiopian tribesmen at Ual-Ual in Italian Somaliland. The L/35 as well as the L/33 was used in Ethiopia and the L/35 equipped the two Italian tank battalions that fought in Spain on Franco's side. Here they came off second best against the Russian T-26 tanks on the Government side. On their return from Spain in 1939 these battalions became the nucleus around which the third armored division, the Littorio, was formed in May 1940. All the battalions of the Littorio and Centauro and one of the Ariete started the war with L3 tankettes. The other two Ariete battalions had M11/39s. The L3/35 was used in Russia by Italian troops who fought there in 1941.

## M Series

While the Carden-Loyd Mark VI gave rise to the L3 series in one direction of development it also influenced the design of the Carro di Rottura (breakthrough tank) which was a turretless vehicle mounting a 47mm gun. In 1937 another Carro di Rottura was produced with a 37mm gun in the hull and a small wedge-shaped turret with a machine-gun. This was the prototype of the M11/39, the first of the medium tank series. (Medium, 11 tons, introduced in 1939). The M11/39 had a Spa 8T V-8 diesel engine of 105hp which gave the tank a maximum speed of 20mph. The range was 125 miles. The engine was rear-mounted with drive sprockets at the front. The 37mm gun was in the front right-hand side of the hull with the driver on the left. In the turret were twin-mounted 8mm Breda machine-guns, fired by the commander of the three-man crew. The suspension consisted of two four-wheel bogie units each side; each group of four wheels was in two pairs, controlled by a single semi-elliptic leaf spring. The M11/39 was 15′6″ long, 7′2″ wide, 7′7″ high. Although mechanically reliable, its main armament being in the hull severely limited its fighting value. Nor did it have a radio. It first saw action at Sidi Azeis on 5 August 1940.

The M11/39 was replaced by the M13/40 which first arrived in Libya in October 1940 and was the backbone of Italian armor in the Desert until after Second Alamein. The M13/40 was a great improvement on its predecessor because it had its main armament, and a more powerful main armament at that, in a fully rotating turret. With the 47mm L/32 Ansaldo gun was a coaxial 8mm Breda 38 machine-gun, and in a twin mounting in

*Original Desert Rats of the 7th British Armoured Division. The tank commander keeps a look-out on his Mark VIA light tank while his crew are busy with personal maintenance.*

the front right of the hull were two more Breda 38s. The M13/40 had a radio unlike the M11/39. Armor maximum was 40mm as against the M11/39's 30mm. The Spa 8T diesel engine was improved to give 125hp. The crew was increased to four. Dimensions were 16′2″ long, 7′3″ wide, and 7′9″ high. The M13/40 first saw action in the Sollum-Halfaya area on 9 December 1940. Over 100 of the tanks were captured in the defeat at Beda Fomm, some of which were used to equip the 6th Royal Tanks. In 1941 a more powerful Spa engine, the 15T, was fitted. This gave 145hp, increased the road speed by two mph and the range by 50 miles. Other improvements were made to the air and fuel filters. With these modifications the tank was designated the M14/41, 14 tons, in fact, being the actual weight of the M13/40. The last development in the series was the M15/42 which was produced in the first two months of 1943. Its 47mm gun had a substantially increased muzzle velocity, and its 15TB gasoline engine with 192hp gave a road speed of 25mph and a range of 175 miles. In March 1943 the M series was wholly replaced in production by the Semoventi self-propelled guns which had been in parallel production on M40-42 chassis since 1941 and which had proved to be an extremely effective weapon against British tanks in the Desert.

*CV L3/35 knocked out in the British attack on Fort Capuzzo, 14 June 1940.*

*M11/39 medium tanks in the Libyan desert. Note 37mm gun in front of hull, machine-gun in turret.*

*M13/40 medium tanks in late 1941. Note 47mm gun in turet, twin machine-guns in hull front.*

## L6/40

To replace the L3 series Fiat and Ansaldo developed a light tank from their earlier 5-ton tanks of 1936-38. This was issued to the Italian army in 1940-41 as the L6/40. Powered by a 68hp Spa engine, with torsion bar suspension, and equipped with a turret mounting a 20mm gun and coaxial 8mm machine-gun, the L6/40 was a considerable improvement on the L3. Armor was increased to 30mm and weight to 6.8 tons. Length 12′ 5″, width 6′ 4″, height 6′ 8″. Speed remained the same at 26mph but range was increased from 75 to 125 miles. However with a two-man crew and only a 20mm main armament it was not a particularly successful combat vehicle. The first L6 units were formed in 1942 with cavalry personnel (later with bersaglieri) and were employed in the Desert and in Russia. They were also issued to units in Greece, France, and Italy.

## P40

It was the intention that the medium tanks should have the support of heavier tanks, just as the Panzer IV was originally to be the support for the Panzer III. The proposed ratio was one company of heavy to three of medium in a tank battalion. This heavy tank was the P40, weighing 26 tons and armed with a 75mm gun and a machine-gun in the front hull. It had a 420 hp engine giving it a speed of 25 mph. It was 18′9″ long, 9′ wide, 8′3″ high, had a crew of four, maximum armor of 60 mm, and a range of 170 miles. By the time Italy surrendered in September 1943 no P40 had been issued to the Italian army, but a number were subsequently completed and used by the Germans at Anzio in 1944.

*Three Italian M11/39s and one M13/40 captured at Bardia, manned by 6th Australian Divisional Cavalry Regiment during the Tobruk operations January 1941. Kangaroo was the divisional sign.*

## British Armored Forces

During World War II the British raised thirty armored brigades. Some were employed in armored divisions, others were used independently. At the beginning of the war there were two armored brigades in each armored division, but after the spring of 1942 they were reduced to one.* The final organization of an armored division was one armored reconnaissance regiment, one armored brigade of three armored regiments and one infantry motor battalion, one lorried infantry brigade of a machine-gun company and three lorried infantry battalions, divisional artillery consisting of a field regiment of 25-pounders, a motorized regiment of self-propelled 25-pounders, an anti-tank regiment and an anti-aircraft regiment, plus engineers, signals, and services.

At the maximum there were eleven armored divisions (1st, 2nd, 6th, 7th, 8th, 9th, 10th, 11th, Guards, 42nd, and 79th). Of these six fought in North Africa, and of the armored brigades 14, some of them in armored divisions, some attached in support of infantry divisions.

The cruiser tanks A9, A10 and A13 were the main striking power of the British armored divisions until they were replaced by the Crusader (Cruiser Mark VI) which first saw action in Operation Battleaxe in June 1941 when the Western Desert Force failed to dislodge Rommel from the Halfaya Pass in an abortive attempt to relieve Tobruk.

## Covenanter

However, before the Crusader came the A13 Mark III (Cruiser Mark V) better known by its name of Covenanter, which began its design life as a "heavy cruiser" project in succession to the A14 and A16. The first deliveries were made in the summer of 1940 and production continued until January 1943 by which time 1,365 Covenanters had been produced in four marks, including some close support tanks with a 3 inch howitzer and a few special purpose tanks (bridgelayers, command, OP, and ARV). The Covenanter weighed 18 tons, had a maximum of 40mm armor, and was armed with a 2 pounder and a coaxial Besa. Its engine was a Meadows Flat 12 of 300 hp giving a speed of 30mph. It was 19' long, 8'7" wide, and 7'4" high, with a crew of four. The author's main recollection of the Covenanter's characteristics is the turret hatch. In most tanks turret hatches were hinged or swivelled round to open. In the Covenanter the hatch which was the full width of the turret lifted back on two struts on to the same plane as the turret top covering the wireless bustle at the back. It was held there by a catch. If the catch gave way, which it frequently did, the tank commander with his head out of the turret would get the full weight of the hatch in the back of the neck — as the author learnt to his cost!

Apart from a Covenanter bridgelayer used by the Australians on Bougainville Island the Covenanter was used for training only and was never in action. It formed a major part of the AFV equipment of the 1st Polish Armoured Division in Scotland and the Guards Armoured Division during their training and of the 9th Armoured Division.

*A brigade in the British army is equivalent to a regiment in, for example, the United States and German armies. A British regiment is equivalent to a battalion.

*Italian L6/40 Light tank.*

*L6/40 in France, 1942.*

*Semovente 75/18 howitzer on M42 chassis.*

*Covenanters (Cruiser Mark V) of the 9th British Armoured Division.*

*Crusader being loaded on to a transporter in the Desert.*

*Mark VI Triumphant! A Light tank of 3rd The King's Own Hussars of 7th Armoured Division (The Deset Rat) with a captured Italian flag after the battle of Beda Fomm, February 1941.*

## Crusader

Almost simultaneously with the Covenanter the next mark of cruiser was developed. The Covenanter design was accepted for production in April 1939, and in August Nuffields' own proposal for a "heavy cruiser" developed from the A13 was accepted. This Cruiser Mark VI was named Crusader. It became the standard British tank of the armored brigades in action in North Africa until replaced by the American Grants and Shermans. From its appearance on the battlefield in June 1941 it continued in service until the end of the North African campaign, with the Sherman gradually replacing it as the Eighth Army moved westwards after the Second Battle of Alamein.

As many Crusaders were produced as all the other cruisers put together. Its total was 4,350 gun tanks plus 1,373 for special roles (command, OP, anti-aircraft, ARV, gun tractor, and bulldozer). The Crusader had a Liberty engine as in the original A13. It was 19'8" long, 8'8" wide, and 7'4" high. Its Christie-type suspension had five road wheels as against the four on the A13s. There were three marks of Crusader: Mark I weighed 18.8 tons, had 40mm of armor at the maximum, and was armed with a 2 pounder and two Besas — one coaxial, the other in a forward sub-turret (this gun and turret were sometimes removed in the field); Mark II was up-armored to 49mm maximum. Both Marks had a crew of five: driver, front gunner, commander, loader/wireless operator, and gunner. The Mark III had a 6 pounder and only the coaxial Besa. It was up-armored to 51mm maximum, weighed 19.75 tons, and had a crew of three: driver, loader/commander in the right of the turret, and gunner. Some specialist Crusaders remained in service after the gun tanks had been withdrawn in May 1943 at the end of the campaign in North Africa.

## Infantry ("I") Tanks

The pilot model of the first "I" tank, the A11 Infantry Tank Mark I, appeared in September 1936. Weighing 11 tons it had a maximum of 65mm armor

*Crusader of 9th Queen's Royal Lancers, 1st Armoured Division in the Desert. The 1st was one of six British divisions that fought in North Africa.*

*Infantry Tank Mark I – the original Matilda – fought in France in 1940.*

*Infantry Tanks Mark II – Matildas attacking in the Desert.*

*Infantry Tanks Mark II – Valentines of 6th British Armoured Division lined up for inspection in September 1941.*

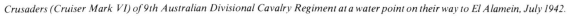

*Crusaders (Cruiser Mark VI) of 9th Australian Divisional Cavalry Regiment at a water point on their way to El Alamein, July 1942.*

*Matilda, Infantry Tank Mark I of the 4th Royal Tank Regiment in France, January 1940.*

but was armed with only a Vickers .303 inch machine-gun. Later this was replaced by a .5 inch mg in some troop leaders' tanks. This heavily armored, under-gunned two-man tank was a curious looking machine with a small plain hull, a one-man turret, and exposed tracks — so curious indeed that it was given the nick-name of Matilda because of its duck-like appearance. It was designed to support infantry in the assault, and 140 were built. Powered by a 70hp Ford V-8 engine it had a top speed of 8mph. The engine was at the rear and drove rear sprockets. The suspension was similar to the Vickers 6-ton tank which influenced design in many countries in the decade before World War II. The A11 was 15'11" long, 7'6" wide, and 6'1½" wide.

While production was beginning on this first Matilda the design of its successor was under way. The pilot model of the A12 Infantry Tank Mark II (sometimes

called "Matilda senior" until the Mark I went out of service after Dunkirk in June 1940 when it formally took over the name Matilda) was ready in April 1938. But by the outbreak of war in September 1939 only two "Matilda seniors" were in service as against 65 Mark Is.

## Matilda

Compared with its predecessor which formed the greater part of the strength of the two infantry tank battalions in the BEF in 1940, "Matilda senior" was altogether a more impressive and important tank. Looking at the Matilda which is now preserved in the Imperial War Museum in London one may be aston-ished at the use of such epithets, but in its day, which lasted for almost two years it was a world-beater. It was the tank which in the hands of the 4th and 7th Royal Tank Regiments set the German SS Totenkopf and 7th Panzer Divisions back on their heels at Arras on 21 May 1940, and in the hands of these same units among others, had many sig-nal successes in the Western Desert.

The Matilda was produced by locomotive builders at the Vulcan Foundry in Warrington, Lancashire, and its solid, robust construction proclaimed its origin. Matilda weighed 26.5 tons with a maximum of 78mm armor. Its dimensions were 18'5" long, 8'6" wide, and 8' high. It was armed with a 2 pounder and a Vickers .303 inch mg (in the case of the first mark) or a 7.92mm Besa (in the case of later marks). The crew of four consisted of commander, gunner, loader/operator, and driver.

Infantry Tank Mark II (Matilda I) and Mark IIA (Matilda II) had two AEC engines, Mark IIA Star (Matilda III) and Mark IIA Double Star (Matildas

*Matildas of the 2/4th Australian Armoured Regiment proved very effective in repelling Japanese attacks on forward infantry positions in close jungle conditions on Bougainville Island, April 1945.*

0'　　　　　5'

## PANZERKAMPFWAGEN IV Ausführung F2

This up-gunned version of Germany's famed Panzer IV, armed with the long 7·5 cm. K L/43, appeared from March 1942 as a hurried answer to the Soviet T-34. It gave the Panzer IV a new lease of life which, with the L/48, saw it through to the end of the war; this version was known to the Allies as the "Mark IV Special". Some of these tanks were operated by the 15th and 21st Panzer Divisions in North Africa, and they played an important part in the German operations at Alam Halfa and El Alamein in September and October 1942.

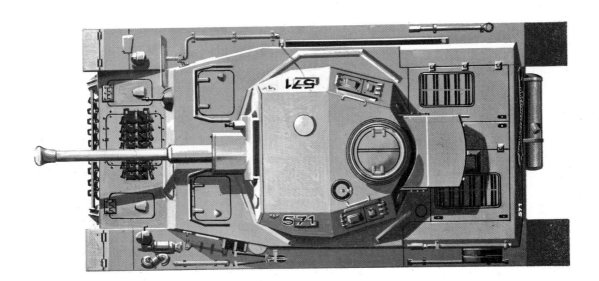

Char B1 *bis*

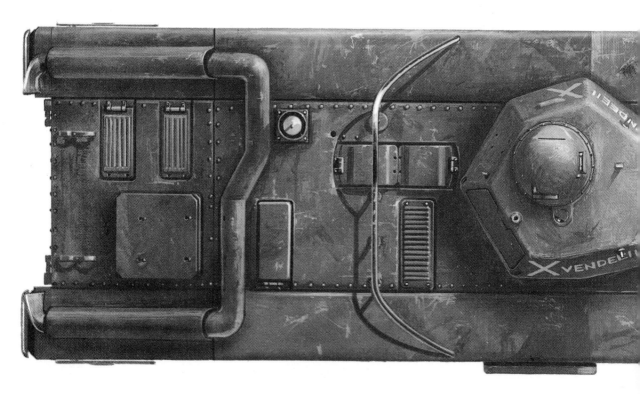

0                                          7 ft

0                                          2m

**Panzer III. Ausf J. of the 3rd Panzer Division. Russian Front, 1941**

A

C

Panzer III. Ausf E. of the 15th Panzer Division, Afrika Korps, 1942.
Battalion HQ vehicle.

A.  Bear emblem of 3rd Pz Div.
B.  Alternative style seen on
    some vehicles.
C.  Tactical marking of
    3rd Pz Div.
D.  Insignia of the Afrika
    Korps.

0´                          5´

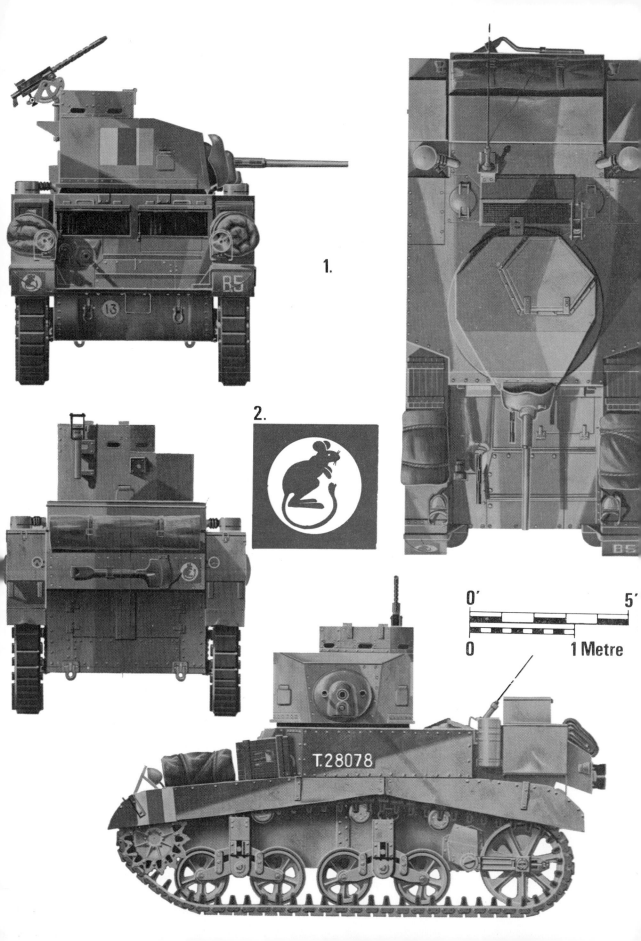

1.

2.

0′       5′

0       1 Metre

T.28078

3.

1 Stuart Mk 1 (Light Tank M3) of 8th King's Royal Irish Hussars, 4th Armoured Brigade, 7th Armoured Division, Battle of Sidi Rezegh, November 1941

2 Formation sign of 7th Armoured Division ('Desert Rats')

3 Light Tank M3A1 of U.S. Marine Corps, Gualdacanal Island, Solomons, September 1942

4 Light Tank M1A1 (formerly Combat Car M2), personal command vehicle of Major General George S. Patton, Commanding General U.S. 2nd Armored Division, Summer 1940

5 Insignia of major general, U.S. Army mounted on right track cover

6 Emblem of U.S. 2nd Armored Division

4.

5.

6.

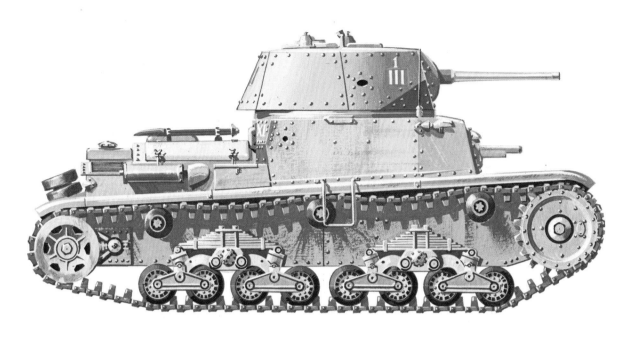

**FIAT-ANSALDO M 13/40**

This tank stands today as a memorial in the Western Desert on Hill 33 at El Alamein. In this painting it carries the insignia of Tank No. 1, 3rd Ptn., 2nd Coy., XI Bn.

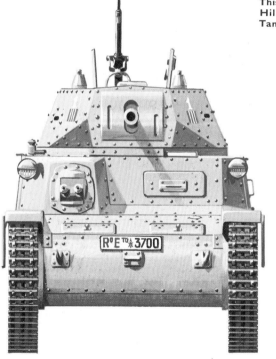

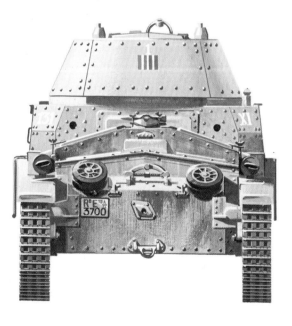

*Valentines of the 8th Royal Tank Regiment, 1st Tank Brigade, before the storming of Bardia, January 1942.*

IV and V) had two Leyland engines. Matildas IV and V had the No 19 wireless set instead of the No 11 set. There was a close support Matilda III and IV with a 3 inch howitzer instead of the 2 pounder. There were also specialized Matildas including Scorpions I and II, Barons, and Anti-mine Roller Attachments for sweeping paths through minefields, CDL tanks for dazzling the enemy in night operations, Matilda with Carrot carrying a demolition charge on the Anti-mine Roller Attachment, and Matilda Frog with flame-throwing equipment in the turret of a Matilda IV. Total production of Matildas was 2,987 before a halt was called in August 1943.

As well as the 4th and 7th RTR in France, Egypt and Cyrenaica, other units with Matildas were the 42nd and 44th RTR (Egypt and Cyrenaica). A squadron of the 4th RTR was in Eritrea with the 4th Indian Division and a half squadron of the 7th RTR was lost in Crete. Detachments from the 6th, 42nd and 44th RTR with Matilda Scorpions were at the Second Battle of Alamein in October 1942. By this time Matilda gun tanks had been withdrawn from the Desert battlefield after a stand at El Alamein in July 1942 when the retreat from Gazala was halted. But the Matilda's service was not finished yet: many were sent to Russia, others were used by the Australians in the Pacific theatre. It was the Australians who developed the Matilda Frog and used it in Borneo in 1945.

## Valentine

Infantry Tank Mark III, the Valentine, was produced in far greater numbers than any other British tank. The first Valentine, built by Vickers-Armstrongs and based on elements of their three earlier tanks — the A9, the A10 and the A11 — came off the production line in May 1940. By the time production ceased early in 1944, 6,855 Valentines (including special vehicles on Valentine chassis) had been built in the United Kingdom, plus 1,420 built in Canada, bringing the grand total to 8,275.

There were eleven marks of the tank. Some had a three-man crew (commander/loader/operator, gunner, and driver), others a four man crew with a loader/operator in the turret as well as the commander and gunner. All had the same "slow motion" three-wheel bogie suspension. The main differences between them were:

| | |
|---|---|
| Mark I | — AEC gasoline engine, two-man turret mounting a 2 pounder and a coaxial Besa mg. |
| Mark II | — as I except for AEC diesel engine. |
| Mark III | — as II except for three-man turret. |
| Mark IV | — as II except for General Motors diesel engine. |
| Mark V | — as IV except for three-man turret. |
| Mark VI | — Canadian Valentine like Mark IV but with Browning .30 inch mg instead of Besa and nose plate cast not bolted. |
| Mark VII | — Canadian Valentine, improved Mark VI. |
| Mark VIII | — AEC diesel engine, two-man turret mounting a 6 pounder only. |
| Mark IX | — Mark VIII except for General Motors diesel engine. |
| Mark X | — Up-rated General Motors diesel engine, two-man turret mounting a 6 pounder and coaxial Besa mg. |
| Mark XI | — as X but with 75mm gun instead of 6 pounder. |

Valentines were used in a number of special roles. The first production DD "swimming" tanks were adaptations of Valentines Marks V, IX and XI; 635 were converted to this role. Valentine DD tanks were used for training in the United Kingdom, Italy, and India. A few were used operationally in Italy in 1945. Valentines were used in tank flame-thrower experiments, as bridge-layers, and with various mine-clearing devices including Scorpion and Snake, the latter being a long tube of explosive pushed across a minefield by the tank and then exploded by remote control to clear a path. There was also a Valentine OP tank, a Valentine Dozer, and a

45

*Infantry tanks Mark III – Valentines of 6th British Armoured Division on the road from Thala to Kasserine to help stem the German breakthrough under Rommel, Tunisia, 19 February 1943.*

few Valentines were converted to CDL (armored searchlight) tanks. The Bishop and the Archer self-propelled guns were on Valentine chassis.

The Valentine weighed 16—17 tons (according to mark) and had a maximum armor thickness of 65mm. It was 17′ 9″ long, 8′ 7½″ wide, and 7′ 5½″ high. Although designed as an infantry tank and used in service as such by tank brigades whose role was the close support of infantry it was also issued to many armored regiments in 1941 instead of cruiser tanks which were in short supply. Despite the different classification there was no real contradiction in this because the Valentine was essentially an improved version of the A10 "heavy" cruiser. Valentines were issued to the 20th and 26th Armoured Brigades of 6th Armoured Division, to the 23rd and 24th Armoured Brigades of 8th Armoured Division, to the 29th and 30th Armoured Brigades of 11th Armoured Division, and to the 1st Polish Armoured Division which was formed in Scotland.

Of these formations the 23rd and 26th Armoured Brigades took Valentines into action, the former fighting in them from First Alamein in July 1942 until the end of the North African campaign, the latter, with Tunisia from November 1942 until the end of February when its units were re-equipped with Shermans. Valentines were first used in action by the 8th RTR of 1st Army Tank Brigade in the attack on Capuzzo on 22 November 1941 during Operation Crusader, and they equipped the same unit in the brigade's famous night attack with the 2nd South African Division against the Bardia fortress on 1 January 1942. The 4th and 44th RTR were also equipped with Valentines later in the Desert campaign, while the 7th RTR took over some Valentines (and five Grants) to add to its remaining Matildas before joining the ill-fated Tobruk garrison with the 4th RTR in June 1942. The 42nd RTR also had a proportion of Valentines at one stage.

Valentines were used by the New Zealand Tank Squadron 3rd Division in the Solomon Islands, by a Special Service Tank Squadron in Madagascar, and, extensively, by the Russians who were sent all but 30 of the Canadian Valentine output plus 1,300 British-built Valentines — a total of 2,690 of which some 400 were sunk en route.

Valentines were also used for a time by the 50th Indian Tank Brigade, but only eight gun tanks were ever in action. On 30 January 1943 during the first Arakan campaign a half squadron of 146 Regiment RAC was landed on the Mayu Peninsula some miles north of Donbaik where a strong Japanese position constructed in great depth had resisted attack after attack by 14th Indian Infantry Division and was preventing them from reaching their final objective at Foul Point. The half squadron of Valentines consisting of two troops and two HQ tanks was commanded by Captain Da Costa, a friend of mine who was commissioned with me from the RAC OCTU at Sandhurst in May 1941. With his two troop leaders, Lieutenants Carey and Thornton, Da Costa reconnoitred the Donbaik position the next day. The recce showed without doubt that the task was too great for only eight tanks. What was needed was a full regimental attack. However the rest of the regiment was in India, so the eight tanks would have to do what they could.

The plan was for the two troops to fight their way through the enemy position, then turn right towards the sea and return along the beach. Da Costa's two HQ tanks would be committed as required. Thornton's troop penetrated the defences first, turned right, and then crashed into an unseen ditch where they were trapped. Carey's troop eventually reached the beach after suffering casualties. Here one of the tanks broke down and had to be towed out of action by Da Costa.

Da Costa then took three tanks along the beach to try to rescue Thornton's troop. As he turned inland an intense artillery barrage made further advance impossible. A rescue attempt by infantry also failed. Thornton's troop was never seen again until two years later when the Mayu was cleared. Carey found the three tanks as they had crashed, "one lying on the after part of another, with the third close by. The guns were still in position," the regimental history records, "and a shell was found in the breech of one of them; but other equipment, such as wireless sets, had been removed." It was not possible to identify the remains of five men found near the tanks.

Apart from the inadequacy of the force the Donbaik attack highlights one of the deficiencies of the Valentine. When closed down the commander's vision was almost non-existent. As the driver depended on the commander for directions in difficult going it was easy enough to fall foul of unseen ditches and other obstacles. Although no other Valentine gun tanks were used in Burma the bridgelayer was in great demand.

## Churchill

Second only to the Valentine in numbers produced was the Infantry Tank Mark IV, the Churchill. The first batch of Churchills came off the Vauxhall Motors production line in June 1941. Ten companies as well as Vauxhall ultimately formed the Churchill Tank Production Group as well as a host of sub-contractors. Production lasted as long as the war and 5,640 Churchills were built. There were a large number of basic marks and variants, but all were powered by a Bedford twin-six 350hp engine giving a maximum speed of 15mph (12.5mph Mark VII), the same as the Valentine and the Matilda. Weight was 39 tons with maximum armor of 102mm on the earlier marks, and 40 tons with a maximum of 152mm on Marks VII and VIII. The dimensions were 24′ 5″ long, 10′ 8″ wide (11′ 4″ Mark VII), and 8′ 2″ high (9′ Mark VII). There was a crew of five.

The main characteristics of the different marks and variants were:

Mark I — 3 inch howitzer in the front hull and a 2 pounder gun with coaxial 7.92mm Besa in cast turret.

Mark II — 3-inch howitzer replaced by Besa.

Mark IICS — as I but with 3-inch howitzer in the turret and 2 pounder in the nose.

Mark III — 6 pounder and coaxial 7.92mm Besa in welded turret and Besa in nose.

Mark IV — as III but with welded turret.

Mark IV (NA75) — IV with 6 pounder replaced by M3 75mm gun from salvaged Sherman: 120

*Churchill AVRE was a Churchill III or IV with a spigot mortar in place of the main armament.*

Mark IVs converted by 21st Tank Brigade workshops in North Africa.

Mark V — as IV but with 95mm howitzer instead of 6 pounder.

Mark VI — as IV but with British-built dual purpose (HE/AP) 75mm gun.

Mark VII — a largely re-designed Churchill with thicker armor, a new cast/welded turret with cupola, circular (instead of square) escape doors on the sides of the hull, five- instead of four-speed gearbox, improved suspension, 75mm gun.

Mark VIII — close support version of VII with 95mm howitzer in place of 75mm gun.

Mark IX — III or IV re-worked to contemporary standards of protection by addition of appliqué armor and by fitting VII's turret though retaining 6 pounder.

Mark IX LT — as IX but with original III or IV turret (LT = Light Turret).

Mark X — VI re-worked as IX but with 75mm gun.

Mark X LT — as X but with original VI turret.

Mark XI — V re-worked as VIII.

Mark XI LT — as XI but with original V turret.

*Infantry Tank Mark IV – Churchill Mark I with 3-inch howitzer in hull front.*

Independent suspension was used throughout with 11 bogies each side, all with triple helical springs except the last on each side which had only a single spring. Bogie diameter was 13 inches.

Churchills were converted for a number of special roles, notably as recovery vehicles, AVREs (Armoured Vehicles, Royal Engineers), and Crocodiles (flame-throwing tanks). AVREs, which were Churchill IIIs or IVs armed with petards and modified to allow the fitting of various devices for demolishing, bridging, or making a passage through anti-invasion defences, equipped the 1st Assault Brigade, RE, of 79th Armoured Division for the North-West Europe campaign, and were also used by the 25th Armoured Assault Brigade in Italy.

Crocodiles were Churchill VIIs with flame-throwing equipment; 31st Armoured Brigade of 79th Armoured Division was the Crocodile brigade, and there were Crocodiles in 25th Armoured Assault Brigade. The 7th RTR, one of the units in 31st Armoured Brigade, used Crocodiles again in the Korean War. Churchills were also widely used as bridgelayers and as ARKs (Armoured Ramp Carriers) for spanning defence ditches or climbing sea walls.

The Churchill first saw action on 19 August 1942 when the Calgary Regiment of 1st Canadian Army Tank Brigade was part of the 2nd Canadian Infantry Divisional Group that assaulted Dieppe. Six Churchills were sent to Egypt to join Eighth Army and took part in the Second Battle of Alamein. Their presence there was for technical evaluation and for propaganda purposes. They absorbed a tremendous amount of punishment in the two actions in which they fought

*Churchill Crocodile in action.*

(Kidney Ridge and Tel el Aqqaqir), receiving 105 hits by armor piercing projectiles alone. One vehicle was burned out, one had track damage, and one a jammed turret. Seven men were killed and eight wounded.

It was not until the Tunisian campaign that Churchills were used in strength over a period of time. Two tank brigades of Churchills were part of First Army. The first of these, 25th Tank Brigade, arrived in the theatre of operations in February 1943 and within twenty-four hours of reaching its concentration area west of Le Kef it found itself preparing for action: the Germans had advanced from the Faid Pass, broken through the Americans at Sidi Bou Zid, and had captured Sbeitla; the whole southern front was wide open.

Churchills of 142 (Suffolk) Regiment, RAC were hurried down from Le Kef to Sbiba and fought their first action in support of 2nd Coldstream Guards, 1st Guards Brigade, to the east of the Sbiba-Sbeitla road at 1700 hours on 21 February.

The second tank brigade to arrive in Tunisia was the 21st Tank Brigade which landed between 23 and 27 March as the third brigade of 4th Infantry Division which was a "mixed" division with one tank and two infantry brigades. Both tank brigades subsequently fought in the Italian campaign, though they were not completely equipped with Churchills throughout.

In the North-West Europe campaign 34th Tank Brigade was equipped with Churchills as were 31st Tank (later Armoured) Brigade (which started with one Crocodile unit and two ordinary Churchill units and ended with three Crocodile units) and 6th Guards Tank Brigade. A few Churchills were also used (though not in action) by the Australians in New Guinea, and on 28 April 1945 a Churchill arrived at Allanmyo in Burma for field trials while the town was being successfully stormed by the Gurkhas and A Squadron of the Carabiniers in their Lees.

The Churchill's principal virtues were its thick armor and its matchless climbing ability which enabled it to reach places where the enemy had thought it impossible for tanks to go. Its drawback was its slow speed. Major-General G. L. Verney has written of it: "I, and others who had the good fortune to fight in Churchill tanks, will always maintain that the Churchill was the best all-round tank this side of the Iron Curtain."

*Churchill adapted for use as a Crocodile. The flame gun can be seen between the horns of the tank with the fuel trailer being towed behind.*

*Panzer IIIs as far as the eye can see; an Ausf J with an H (left) leads a company of tanks forward during the victorious sweep into Russia, summer 1941.*

# IV
# 1941—45: German Campaign Against
the Soviet Union

On 22 June 1941 Germany attacked the Soviet Union. It was the first anniversary of the German armistice with France. The German order of battle had three Army Groups with panzer divisions as the spearhead of each. Their chief tank was the Panzer III.

To meet this invasion the Russians had, as far as armor was concerned, some 20,000 tanks of which about 1,600 were the excellent T-34 medium and KV-1 heavy, both armed with a high velocity 76.2mm gun 30.5 calibers long capable of firing both HE and AP rounds. The majority of the Russian tanks, however, were not up to the high technical standard of the T-34 and the KV-1, many of them being survivors from the early days of Russian tank production. There were a large number of T-26 light tanks and BT fast cruiser tanks, the latter being the predecessors of the T-34. There were also some heavy tanks of ponderous design. BTs and T-26s were 75 per cent of the Soviet tank strength.

The Germans correctly estimated the number of Russian tanks, although curiously enough their intelligence had discovered nothing of the existence of the T-34s and KVs, although admittedly these had been built and issued to units in the utmost secrecy. The Russians on the other hand considerably over-estimated the German tank strength, reckoning that it amounted to 15-18,000 which in terms of "runners" meant several times the Russian number because on the eve of Germany's attack 29 per cent of the older Soviet tanks required major overhauls and 44 per cent needed nor-

mal service overhauls — that is, more than half the tank force needed servicing.

With 20,000 tanks the Russians had more than all the other tank forces in the world put together. Of these 20,000 about 7,000 were in the forward areas, but conscious of the number of their tanks needing servicing and imagining that they were opposed by 15,000 or more, the Russians considered themselves to be heavily outnumbered. In point of fact the Germans attacked with 2,434 tanks, excluding what General von Thoma, then head of the tank side of the General Staff, called the "sardine tins". Including them the total was about 3,200. As an example of this disparity and misconception: on the southern front FM von Kleist, who led FM von Rundstedt's panzer drive, had only 600 tanks; opposing him was Marshal Budenny's Army Group with 2,400. Before and during World War II the German armor strength was continually over-estimated, thanks partially to a most effective propaganda campaign and partially to the great tactical skill with which those tanks available in the field were used so that they always seemed to be many more than they actually were. One of the most skilful armor tacticians in achieving this was General Balck whose career included command of the 1st Rifle Regiment in 1st Panzer Division and subsequently command of 11th Panzer Division (the Ghost Division), 48 Panzer Corps, 4th Panzer Army, and Army Group G.

At the time of the German attack, Operation Barbarossa was its code-name, the Russians were in the

*Panzer II Ausf. Bs in Russia.*

process of changing the organization of their armored troops. Originally they had regarded tanks simply as close support for infantry. Then in the mid-thirties, linked to the struggle for supremacy within the ruling hierarchy, the ideas of Liddell Hart and Fuller gained ground despite bitter opposition and were crystallized in the 1936 Field Service Regulations. The principal protagonist of this mobile concept was S. M. Kirov. But Russia in the 1930s was a much more dangerous place to have novel ideas about the use of tanks than Britain. At least Fuller, Pile, Broad, Martell and the other British armor enthusiasts were only sent into military exile. Kirov was shot by a firing squad!

Experience in the Spanish Civil War where Russian T-26s were used, together with the realization that Soviet industry could not produce sufficient suitable tanks to implement the policy of independent operations by a predominantly tank force, swung the pendulum

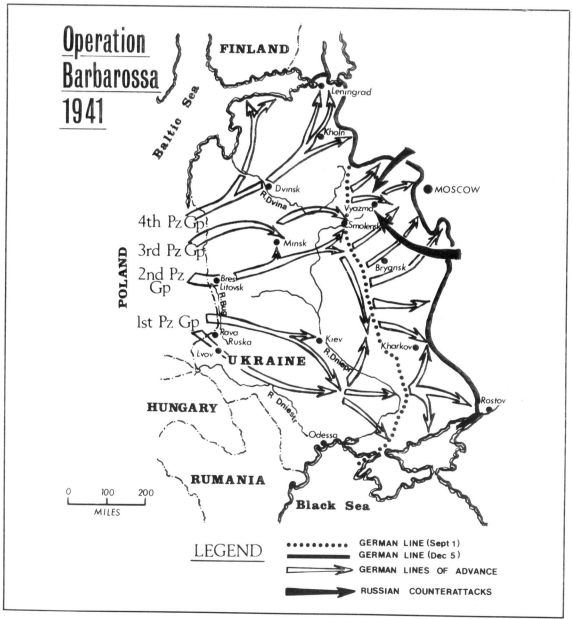

# Operation Barbarossa 1941

FINLAND

Baltic Sea

Leningrad

Kholn

Dvinsk

R.Dvina

MOSCOW

Vyazma

Smolensk

POLAND

4th Pz Gp

3rd Pz Gp

Minsk

2nd Pz Gp

Brest Litovsk

R.Bug

Bryansk

1st Pz Gp

Rava Ruska

Lvov

UKRAINE

Kiev

R.Dniepr

Kharkov

R Dniestr

Rostov

HUNGARY

Odessa

RUMANIA

Black Sea

0   100   200
MILES

LEGEND

• • • • • • • •  GERMAN LINE (Sept 1)
―――――――  GERMAN LINE (Dec 5)
▭―――▷  GERMAN LINES OF ADVANCE
■―――▶  RUSSIAN COUNTERATTACKS

*Russian KV-1A heavy tank. Note the vision slit immediately above a pistol port in the side of the turret.*

back in 1940 to using tanks principally in support of infantry formations. Hardly had this policy been decided upon, however, when German *Blitzkreig* methods in Poland and France caused a change of thought yet again. Two tank divisions and a motorized division were to form a tank corps, the tank division consisting of two tank regiments, an infantry regiment, and a mechanized artillery regiment, the motorized division consisting of one tank regiment, two infantry regiments, and an artillery regiment. The training of these tank corps was in progress when the Germans struck.

Thus, as Colonel Norman has written, "the Soviet Army was in the throes of reorganization, most of the tanks were obsolescent, commanders were unfamiliar with their new tasks, and such armored forces as were available were dispersed linearly across the front without reserves. This piecemeal use of armor was no match for the well-proven *Blitzkreig* techniques, and ... the Soviet nominal superiority of about four to one in tanks was of little avail. By the winter of 1941 there were practically no large armored formations still operational."

With the stabilization of the front in 1941—42 the Russians were able to form new units and their tank industry which had been redeployed beyond the Urals began to make good the losses in equipment. Early in 1942 tank brigades were given a new establishment. Each consisted of three mixed tank battalions, a motorized infantry machine-gun battalion, an anti-tank company, a mortar company, a reconnaissance battalion, and an anti-aircraft battalion. Each mixed tank battalion had 23 tanks. Throughout 1942 and 1943, however, shortage of equipment meant that each brigade only had two tank battalions; a motorized rifle battalion took the place of the third.

Individual tank brigades were grouped into tank corps, three to each corps. The corps also included one motor rifle brigade, one or two heavy tank battalions, self-propelled artillery and anti-tank units, reconnaissance, rocket launcher, mortar, and anti-aircraft battalions. At full strength a tank corps corresponded roughly to a western Allied armored division and had a similar role. Mechanized corps were used to follow up the tanks corps. Independent tank brigades, equipped mainly with T-34s as were the integrated brigades, were used for the support of infantry formations with no generic armored units.

## T-26

The Vickers "Six-Ton" tank has already been mentioned as a vehicle which influenced design in many countries. Although it was not accepted by the British army because of doubts about its suspension, others did take it, especially the Red army which ordered fifteen in 1930 and then built the tank under license as the T-26.

The first models, produced between 1931 and 1933 and known collectively as the T-26A, were almost identical to the Vickers Type A, except that there were a number of variants as regards armament. For example, the T-26A5 had one long 37mm gun in the right-hand turret and an air-cooled machine-gun in the left-hand one; the T-26A2 had two air-cooled machine-guns instead of the water-cooled ones in the T-26A1 — and so on.

Type B models were also built and known as T-26B. From 1933 production was concentrated on this model which was to be used by the cavalry arm; production of T-26As ceased. The short 47mm gun of the Vickers Type B was replaced by a long 45mm L/46 gun of much higher velocity (2,350 feet per second), which gave the T-26B a very useful anti-tank "punch" for a light tank. Its length was 16′ 3″, width 8′, height 8′; it had a 90hp engine, weighed 9.5 tons with maximum armor of 15mm, and had a crew of three. Its maximum speed was 18mph and its range was 190 miles.

In 1937 a new version of the T-26 appeared. Known as the T-26S in the Soviet Union (and usually as the

*Enemy eye-view of a T34/76A with its 76.2mm L/30.5 gun.*

T-26C elsewhere) this had a new slope-sided turret and featured a greater use of welded armor than on the earlier models. Some of these earlier T-26s were retrofitted with the new S type turret. In 1939 production of the T-26 ceased. In all there were probably some 4,500 built.

As well as their numerically important role against the Germans at the outset of the Great Patriotic War the T-26s also saw action in the Spanish Civil War (1936—39) as mentioned earlier, in Manchuria (Khalkin-Gol) in 1938, and in Finland (1939—40).

## Other Russian Light Tanks

As well as the fifteen "Six-Tonners" the USSR also bought from Britain a number of Vickers medium tanks, and some Carden-Lloyd Mark VIs and amphibious light tanks. The Mark VIs were put into production as the T-27, the Vickers Carden-Loyd amphibians gave rise to the T-37 and T-38 light tanks. Both had a crew of two. The T-37 weighed nearly 3 tons and had a 40hp engine which gave it a speed of 22mph on land and 4mph afloat when it was propelled by a reversible screw. It

was armed with a 7.62mm machine-gun. The T-37 was built in quantity from 1932 to 1938 and its successor the T-38 began to appear in 1936.

These light amphibious reconnaissance vehicles were replaced in service in 1941 by the T-40. This and the heavy SMK were the first Soviet tanks to have torsion bar suspension, a system patented in the United States in 1932. The T-40 had four large road wheels and three return rollers each side. It weighed about 6 tons and had 14mm armor. It was powered by a 85hp 6-cylinder GAZ truck engine and had a speed of 28mph on land and 4mph afloat. Its range was 210 miles. It was armed with two machine-guns — a 12.7mm and a 7.62mm. Like the earlier amphibians it had a crew of two. It was 14' long, 7' 8" wide, and 5' 8" high.

Four other light tank types were built by the Soviet Union during the war: the T-50, T-60, T-70, and T-80. The T-50 was not amphibious. It weighed 13.5 tons, had a crew of four, and was armed with a 45mm gun and a 7.62mm machine-gun. It was 17' 4" long, 8' 3" wide, and 7'2" high. The suspension was changed to six double-tired, spoked wheels of smaller diameter than on the T-40. A 300hp engine overcame the additional weight to give an improved speed performance of 32mph. Armor was 37mm maximum.

The T-60 was virtually the same as the T-40 except that it was not amphibious and had a larger turret that mounted a 20mm gun with a coaxial 7.62mm machine-gun. It weighed about the same as the T-40. Maximum armor was 20mm.

The T-70 had two power units arranged in tandem, each of 70hp. To accommodate the engines the turret, carrying a 45mm gun and a coaxial 7.62mm machine-gun, was moved over to the left. Five rubber-tired road wheels and three return rollers together with torsion bar springing were used for the suspension. Its dimensions were about the same as the T-40. Both the T-60 and T-70 had a crew of two, but the weight of the T-70 was considerably greater at 9.2 tons. The T-80, like the T-70, came into service in 1942 and differed from the T-70 in having its turret armor increased to 60mm and

*Three Panzer I Ausf. As in Russia following an early model Panzer III (Ausf. B or C).*

its power units up-rated to 85ph each. A third crew member was added. It weighed 11.6 tons. It was 14' 8" long, 8' 4" wide, and 7' 3" high.

With the T-80 Soviet light tank production ceased until after the war. The T-70 chassis was used to mount a 76.2mm gun as self-propelled artillery, the SU76 (Samokhodnaya Ustanovka).

## BT Series

Of the two most numerous tanks in Russian service in 1941 the first, the T-26, was developed from a British design, the second, the BT-7, was the last in a series whose original design had come from the United States.

Ten years before the beginning of the Great Patriotic War the Soviet Union, as we have seen, adopted, for a time, the "mobile war" philosophy of Fuller and Liddell Hart. To carry these ideas into effect would require fast long-range tanks that could "penetrate to the furthest limits of the whole defensive system, destroy the enemy reserves and HQs and cut off the enemy's retreat. Their actions should be planned," Field Service Regulations continued, "so that the infantry and their supporting tanks, taking advantage of the disorganization effected by the long-range tanks, may move forward and prevent any reorganization of the defense."

The tank chosen for this long-range task was the BT, the initials standing for Bystrochodnij Tankov (Fast Tank). During a visit to the United States and Europe to inspect available armored vehicles under development which might meet the needs of the "mobile war" philosophy, the Soviet special commission was greatly impressed by J. Walter Christie's wheel-cum-track design. Of the nine M1931 Christie chassis that were built five were ordered by the US Army, two by the Polish Government, these two being taken over by the US Army as the T3E1 when the Poles defaulted, and the remaining two were sold under license to the Soviet

*The Russian T-26C (or T-26S) was originally copied from the Vickers Six-Ton tank.*

Union — though, it may be added, Christie never received a royalty from the BTs that resulted from this purchase.

After extensive testing the Revolutionary War Council of the USSR ordered work to begin on modifying the Christie design to meet Soviet requirements. Manufacture of the first model, the BT-1 began in May 1931 and was completed within a month. Two further prototypes to a simplified design were built in August and known as the BT-2.

The BT had a three-man crew. Its general construction, apart from the unique Christie suspension, was conventional for the period. The lay-out was copied from the Christie T3 with the engine and transmission in the rear half, the turret (identical to the Christie turret) centrally placed on the forward part of the hull, and the driving compartment, also centrally placed, at the very front of the tank. The BT, like its Christie prototype could run on either wheels or tracks, the change

*BT-7-2s under the gaze of Lenin's statue in Minsk before the Great Patriotic War which began in June 1941.*

*J. Walter Christie, tank genius, in his M1931 (T-3) medium tank which became the BT-1 and, through the development of the BT series, evolved into the T-34. Christie's similar M1932 design was sold to Britain and became the A13 cruiser prototype.*

from one mode to the other taking about thirty minutes. When running on wheels the drive was transferred from the rear sprockets to the rear road wheels through a chain drive. The tank was steered through the front road wheels instead of the clutch and brake system used when the tank was on tracks. When not in use the tracks were carried on shelves along the sides of the hull. On wheels the BT-7 had a top speed of 45mph and earlier models could reach 70mph. Even on tracks the maximum was 39mph for BT-1 to BT-5 and 33mph for the BT-7. It was its speed rather than its wheel/track capability, which was seldom used, that made the BT so successful. Added to this was its good cross-country ability. These characteristics resulted from the high power to weight ratio of over 30hp/ton and the Christie suspension, which consisted of four large road wheels on each side, revolving on pivoted axle arms. Each wheel had dual rubber tires, and each axle was controlled by a long adjustable coil spring housed vertically inside the hull side plates.

The BT-1 was armed with two machine-guns in the turret. Only one vehicle was built. Production models of the BT-2 had a 37mm gun and one machine-gun. BT-3 had a 45mm gun and a separately ball-mounted DT machine-gun as in the BT-2. Road wheels were solid as opposed to spoked in the BT-2. The BT-4 was an unsuccessful attempt to produce an infantry version of the BT equipped with the twin turret arrangement of the T-26A. These first four BT models were powered by the Liberty 400hp aircraft engine which, with the weight of the BT-2 at 11 tons, gave a power to weight ratio of 36.4.

At the end of 1932 the next model, the BT-5, went into production. This became standard and remained in service until 1941. The turret mounted a 45mm gun and a coaxial machine-gun and carried radio equipment. The muzzle velocity of the gun at 2,350 feet per second was greater than that of all foreign light tanks right up to the outbreak of World War II. The BT-5 turret was simultaneously adopted for the T-26B. The engine was the Soviet designed M-5 12-cylinder aircraft engine adapted for tank use, giving 350hp. A number of special purpose BT-5s were produced.

There was no BT-6 (that is to say it never progressed beyond the paper stage) and the penultimate tank in the series was the BT-7 which went into production in 1935. It was the BT-7 on manoeuvers that aroused great admiration among foreign military observers, among them the British armor expert Martel. With General Wavell, Colonel Martel saw the tanks in Byelorussia in September 1936. "The design of the fighting body," he wrote afterwards, "is not very good but the performance of the machine is at least twice as good as the A9. The suspension is excellent ... We saw several machines pass at 30mph over a prepared bank which had a vertical drop of five feet on the far side. The whole machine leapt through the air and cleared a 30 foot gap. There was no apparent damage to the suspension or the crew. The engine is an aircraft engine of some 300hp output ... and the great advantage of using a really powerful engine is very apparent."

The engine was in fact a new M-17T (also used in the T-28) with an output of 450hp. Martel estimated the

*Early production model of the BT-2 running on wheels. Compare the mantlet with that of the later production model.*

*BT-3: this model had a 45mm gun and a separately ball-mounted DT machine-gun.*

*Later production BT-5 tank with new, rounded mantlet and twin turret hatches.*

armor basis at 16mm — it was in fact 22mm maximum. He concluded his report by suggesting that the British War Office should buy a Russian Christie. "Unless we can improve the A9 to a very considerable extent, I cannot help feeling dismay at the idea of our building any large number of these tanks which will be far inferior to existing Russian tanks."

The early production BT-7s had the old cylindrical turrets of the BT-5. Then a new turret was introduced. It was conical in shape, had twin horn periscopes, and gave greater protection with armor increased from 13mm to 15mm. It was similar to that used on the T-26S. The "cylindrical" tanks were the BT-7-1, the "conical" ones the BT-7-2. It was 18′ 8″ long, 8′ wide, 7′ 6″ high.

The combat service of the BT-7 before the German onslaught of 1941 was in the Khalkin-Gol operations in Manchuria in 1938, the advance into Poland in September 1939, and in the war against Finland in 1939—40.

The last tank in the series was the BT-7M, also known as the BT-8. It weighed 14.6 tons, mounted a 76.2mm

gun, and had several changes in hull and turret arrangement from earlier BT tanks — the glacis plate occupied the full width of the tank and was in the form of an inverted 'V'; a hull machine-gun was installed next to the driver, and ball-mounted machine-guns were located in each side of the turret which was itself different from the other BT ones and more closely resembled that on the T-28 medium. It was used in Khalkin-Gol and in Finland.

### Russian Heavy Tanks

The first heavy tank taken into Red army service was the T-32 in 1930—31. This was a close copy of the British "Independent" tank (A1E1) of 1926. Only one Independent was built but it had an important influence on tank design, not only being reflected in the T-32 and the T-28 medium which is discussed later, but also in the French *Char de Rupture*, the German *Neubaufahrzeug*, and the British medium tanks of the 1926—37 period.

As with the Independent the T-32 had a main turret and four auxiliary turrets, sufficient, it was believed, for it to operate independently on its own. In 1933 an improved version, the T-35, was produced. Both the T-32 and the T-35 had massive slab sides reaching low down on the suspension. The main turret carried a 76.2mm gun, two of the auxiliaries had 7.62mm machine-guns, and the other two had 37mm, later replaced by 45mm guns. Each of the three larger guns also had a coaxial machine-gun. Although the idea of multi-turreted tanks which could engage several targets simultaneously and thus act as mobile fortresses was outmoded before World War II began, production of the T-35 continued until 1939 and some 20 to 30 were built.

Despite this small output there were probably three distinct versions of the T-35: one with an armor basis of 30mm, a second with a new model of the 45mm gun, and a third with an armor basis of 50mm. All three had a 10-man crew (as had the T-32), a 500hp 12-cylinder M-17 gasoline engine situated in the rear half of the hull, giving a maximum road speed of 18mph and a cross-country speed of 12mph. The length was 31′ 6″, width 10′ 6″, height 11′ 3″. Weight varied according to armor basis between 44 and 49 tons.

The T-28 falls between the medium and heavy class, but as it was the main equipment of the heavy tank brigades in the 1930s it may legitimately be included here. It was tested in 1932 and continued in production until 1939. As well as owing something to the Independent it was also strongly influenced by a British medium

*BT-7M; also known as the BT-8, the last in the series. Among other changes the glacis plate, in the form of an inverted 'V', covered the full width of the tank.*

*A column of BT-7-2s. The BT-7-2 had a conical turret similar to that on the T-28S Light Tank.*

*Later model BT-5s on manoeuvres with the cavalry in evidence.*

tank the A6 (known as the "16-Tonner"). Like the A6 it had two auxiliary turrets, each with a machine-gun, on each side of the driver. The T-28's main armament was a 76.2mm howitzer. On each side of this was a machine-gun independently mounted. In the T28-B the howitzer was replaced by a gun of similar caliber. The tank was powered by a M-17L 12-cylinder V of 500hp — a Soviet version of the American Liberty aero engine. This gave a top speed of about 20mph. The weight was 27.5 tons giving a power to weight ratio of 18.2. Suspension was five 4-wheeled bogies each side with a single pair both at the front and the back, controlled by coil springs without shock absorbers. The springs were protected by side plates. Armor maximum was 30mm which was increased to 80mm in a model called the T-28M or T-28C. There was a crew of six. The T-28 was 24′ 9″ long, 9′ 4″ wide, 9′ 4″ high. After taking part in the Spanish Civil War T-28s operated in Finland and,

rather unsuccessfully against the Panzer IIIs and IVs, at the beginning of Barbarossa.

One particular point about the T-28 and T-35 is worth noting. Whereas other nations continued to believe for some years longer that any tank need carry an anti-tank gun no bigger than one of about 37mm caliber, the Soviet Union realised as early as the 1920s that their heavier tanks needed guns of much greater caliber and that HE capability was essential.

T-35s were used, without much success, in the Russian campaign against Finland from December 1939 to March 1940. The only time they came up against the Germans was at Lvov in Poland shortly after Operation Barbarossa had begun. Sadly, the mobile fortresses were immobile for they had run out of fuel.

Three designs for a tank to replace the T-35 were evolved in 1938. The first of these resulted in the SMK,

*T-35A with improved 45mm in two of the four subsidiary turrets. The frame aerial has been removed from the 76mm turret.*

BT-5: commander's model of the BT-5 tank with frame
aerial round the turret roof.

BT-7-2. Note twin horn periscopes on top of turret.

Panzer IIIs of Panzer Group South cross the Don river
during the advance on Stalingrad, summer 1942.

*Panther Ausf. D.*

*A remarkable view of a burning Panther Ausf. A, photographed through the driver's visor of the approaching SU-85 which had just knocked it out, Russian Front, winter 1944.*

*BT-7-1(V) on wheels. Although the frame aerial has been removed the mountings for it on the turret are clearly visible.*

*Three-quarter front view of T-28 in German hands.*

76.2mm L/30.5 gun and three 7.62mm machine-guns — one coaxial, one in the hull left front, and one that was fired from a ball-mount in the turret rear. The KV-1 had a crew of five commander/loader, gunner, and second driver-mechanic in the fighting compartment, and the driver-mechanic and hull gunner/radio operator in the front of the hull, the driver in the center, the gunner on the left. The power plant was a V-2 diesel of 600hp. Suspension was the same torsion bar type that had been used on the SMK and T-100 with six twin steel wheels and three return rollers on each side. The driving sprockets were at the rear. The tracks were unusually wide, 27.5 inches, and this kept ground pressure down to little more than that of the much lighter BT-7. Armor was on a 90mm basis with 110mm maximum. The range was 210 miles and the top speed was given as 22mph, but this speed was somewhat illusory as gears could be shifted easily only when the tank was stationary.

The KV-1 was followed by the 1A, 1B and 1C in 1940 and 1941 (the suffixes were German additions for identification purposes). Each was basically the same as the original, the main difference being added armor which increased the weight to 48 tons in the KV-1C. The KV-1S, which appeared in 1942, was designed for speed. A maximum of 27mph was achieved by reducing armor and bringing the weight down to 42.5 tons. With the introduction of better armored German tanks, especially the Tiger, the effectiveness of the 76.2mm gun was reduced. In the spring of 1943 the KV-85 was brought into service with an 85mm gun. To accommodate the larger turret ring the width of the KV-1S was increased by four inches to 11′ 4″ and the weight crept up again to 46 tons. The length at 22′ 6″ was the same as for the earlier models. Height was 9′ 3″ as against 10′ 8″. The KV-85 like the KV-1C and KV-1S had a cast turret instead of a fabricated one.

named after Kirov who had been posthumously reinstated in official favor. The SMK was given an armor basis of 60mm which raised its weight to 56 tons. Only two turrets were mounted this time, the lower having a 45mm gun, and the upper, behind it, a 76.2mm. In addition there were three 7.62mm machine-guns. The crew was also reduced to seven. The tank had torsion bar suspension. It was powered by a 500hp gasoline engine developed from a German BMW aircraft unit. The second design was for the T-100 which was almost identical to the SMK. Very few of either design were built. It was the third design that flourished.

### The KV Series
This third design was carried out under the leadership of I. S. Kotin. The new tank was named after Marshal of the Soviet Union Klimenti Voroshilov, KV for short. The KV-1 was a 43.5 ton tank armed with a

*KV-1A. Note the upward continuation of the front plate to protect the turret ring.*

*KV-1 C.*

In February 1940 an "artillery tank" version of the KV-1 was first brought into action against the Mannerheim Line in Finland. This was the KV-2 which had a 152mm howitzer mounted in high box-like turret on a KV-1 chassis. The turret with gun weighed 12 tons and the total weight of the tank was 53 tons. Below the turret ring it was identical to the KV-1. The turret crew differed from that in the KV-1 in having a separate commander, gunner, loader, and a spare driver-mechanic who probably helped to manipulate the ammunition. Although a potentially formidable weapon the KV-2 was usually neutralized after being outflanked and it was in due course replaced by the turretless SU-152 which had a height of 8′ against the KV-2's 12′.

*An abandoned KV-2. The bolted-on plate at the rear of the turret covered the aperture necessary to mount the 152mm howitzer.*

## The IS Series

While the KV series was running its course Kotin in 1941 had started a design study aimed at increasing the firepower and protection of a heavy tank without exceeding the weight of the KV-1S. The result was the IS-1, named after Joseph Stalin. There was no machine-gun in the hull, which gave a better ballistic shape for the glacis plate. The suspension remained essentially the same although the sprocket, top rollers and track adjusting wheel were all lowered to allow the construction of panniers over the top run of the tracks and thereby a wide turret ring to accommodate a larger gun. Tanks in the IS series had a crew of four.

A few IS-1As appeared in 1943, some armed with a 85mm gun, others with the same 100mm gun used in the SU-100 tank destroyer. By 1944 these guns had been replaced by the 122mm and the modified vehicles were designated IS-1B. At the same time production of the IS-2 had begun at the Kirov plant in the Urals and the Germans reported their first contact with this tank in

*KV-85. Note the changes in the hull front and the similarity to the IS-1 which followed soon afterwards.*

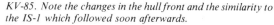

*KV-2. The box-like turret is mounted on a standard KV chassis.*

early 1944. The most obvious difference between the IS-1 and IS-2 was the glacis plate which was now uniformly sloped instead of being bent as in the earlier model. The main armament was the 122mm L/43 gun. There were four machine-guns, one a 12.7mm DShK anti-aircraft, the other three 7.62mm DT — one coaxial, one in the left rear of the turret, and one fired by the driver through an aperture in the glacis plate. The turret was an unsymmetrical casting, the left hand side being near vertical while the right sloped at about 20 degrees. Armor maximum on the turret was 100mm, on the hull 105mm. The engine and transmission was almost unchanged from that in the KV-1. Weight was 45.5 tons, top speed 27mph, range 120 miles. The tank was 21' 10" long, 10' 3" wide, 9' high. Production was 2,350. The IS-2, like the KV-2, was adapted to the SU role.

## T-34

It has frequently been said that the tank which had the greatest impact on the fighting in World War II was the Russian T-34. Its German opponents — Guderian, von Kleist, and von Rundstedt for example, to say nothing of the front-line soldiers who had to face it — were loud in its praise. "The best tank in any army up to 1943," was Guderian's judgement. "The T-34 tank was the finest in the world," said von Kleist; and von Rundstedt agreed with him.

Tanks are like race-horses: breeding counts. The family tree of the T-34 started with the brilliant American inventor and designer J. Walter Christie and his T3

Medium tank which was built in 1931. The outstanding feature of the Christie was its suspension which had large road wheels around which the tracks were driven without return rollers. The center of alternate track shoes carried a 7-inch tongue which engaged a roller in the drive sprocket wheel and also guided the tracks between the split tires of the road wheels. As we have seen with the BT series Christie's system allowed the tank to run in two modes, either on tracks or on wheels.

Christie's aim with this new type of suspension was to give his tank greatly enhanced speed and to allow it to take maximum advantage of the terrain. The wheeled mode would give greater speed than tracks on approach marches over roads or firm steppe country, as well as lessening track wear. The value of the new suspension in the tracked mode would be to allow faster movement across country than the other types of suspension then in vogue.

Mobility was Christie's quest — mobility that could come only from speed. In a brochure called "Modern Mobile Defense" he wrote: "My first object was to build a chassis that would protect the man who is to risk his life by facing the enemy and to provide a machine by the use of which he can defend himself and destroy the enemy. Therefore we built a chassis with frontal lines and slopes that will make it almost impossible to penetrate the chassis with any type of projectile. Next, we constructed the chassis as low as possible, making it as inconspicuous as the power plant permits. We then turned to the next problem of defense

*IS-2 heavy tanks in Cuban service parading past Fidel Castro in Havana, 1961. The IS-2 had a uniformly sloping glacis plate compared with the bent plate on the IS-1. There was a change also in the driver's vision device.*

*A representative T-34/76B with a "long" 76.2mm gun, 41.2 calibers. Armor thickness is improved but standard turret* *fittings of the "A" model are retained including side episcopes, pistol ports, back plate and single, forward opening roof hatch.*

*T34/76A – The first version of the medium tank that replaced the BT series and which was to be considered by no less an authority than Guderian as "the best tank in any army up to 1943".*

which is speed. Speed in an aeroplane or speed on the ground is equally important. With speed you can surround the enemy, you can outflank him, you can reach points quickly and take up positions to stop the advance. If you meet an overpowering force you can quickly evade it."

Realising that the BT series was not sufficiently armored to withstand modern anti-tank fire and that their heavy tanks were too slow Soviet designers turned to the fast medium tank which retained the basic Christie features, One of the first was the A-20 of 1938. Weighing 18 tons, with maximum armor of 25mm and armed with a 45mm gun, plus one turret and one hull machine-gun, the A-20 was a direct predecessor of the T-34 as its shape reveals — over-hanging hull, sharply inclined side and glacis plates, and small well-angled turret. The A-20, which was powered by a 450hp diesel engine giving a top speed of 50mph, still had the wheel-cum-track capability of the BT series. In 1939 it was up-gunned with a 76.2mm and became the A-30.

In the T-32, also produced in 1939, the wheel mode was discarded. Apart from this the T-32 was essentially similar to the A-30, but with armor increased to 45mm and the number of road wheels increased to five each side.

From the T-32 to the T-34 there was a short step in design terms. The two prototype T-34s were given an arduous trial run from Kharkov to Moscow and back in March 1940. The designer-in-chief was M. I. Koshkin, who died of illness in September 1940. A. A. Morozov led the group responsible for the transmission system, while the notable configuration of the hull and its armor plating was developed by N. A. Kucherenko and M. I. Tarshinov. The well-sloped plates offered the maximum resistance to attack and were "a characteristic noticeably lacking in contemporary German and British vehicles with their slab-sided hulls and turrets," as J. M. Brereton has pointed out. Not until the Panther, their answer to the T-34, did the Germans attempt anything similar. A weakness, however, was the rear overhang of the cramped two-man turret which the

*In action on the Eastern Front 1943, these T-34/76 Bs show the modified turret with twin hatches for commander/gunner and loader. Note absence of pistol ports in turret sides, also non-standard stowage bins at rear. The grab rails on turret and hull sides (for infantry) were also a modification.*

Germans found very convenient for fixing Teller mines to and blowing off the turret complete.

The first production T-34 appeared in June 1940. It was built at Kharkov. Other factories engaged on T-34 production were at Leningrad and Stalingrad. When the Germans overran Kharkov and besieged Leningrad the plants were evacuated to Chelyabinsk east of the Urals where they formed what became known as Tankograd, the largest tank engineering combine in the Soviet Union. At Stalingrad T-34 production con-

*The IS-1 heavy tank.*

*This T-34/76 with modified turret shows an odd combination of early type of perforated steel-tyred wheels with the final rubber-tyred disc type. There was no doubt a spares problem in the field.*

tinued under the muzzles of the enemy guns and the tanks were driven in a "raw" state straight into action off the assembly lines.

The first T-34s were known, in the West at any rate, as the T-34/76A, the 76 signifying the caliber of the main armament, a 76.2mm L/30.5 gun. Maximum armor was 45mm and the weight was 26.3 tons. The engine was a highly important element in the excellence of the T-34. Gasoline engines normally used for automobiles and aircraft were relatively uneconomic when adapted for tanks. To give it sufficient power entailed a

corresponding increase in fuel consumption. This in turn meant bigger fuel tanks, which meant increased size and increased weight. Furthermore there was the fire hazard. For the T-34 a 500hp diesel engine was developed which gave the tank a top speed of 32mph and a power to weight ratio of 17.9hp/ton. The range was 190 miles.

The T-34/76 had a crew of four: commander/gunner and loader in the turret to operate the main armament and the coaxial 7.62mm DT machine-gun, driver, and hull gunner/radio operator who fired the other 7.62mm

*Soviet infantry dismounting from a company of T-34/85s to assault an enemy position in the Odessa area. Reconnaissance troops mounted on motor-cycle combinations are associated with this sub-unit.*

*Four views of a T-34/85 captured in Korea and now in the Royal Armoured Corps Tank Museum, Bovington, Dorset. Noteworthy features are the poor ballistic shape of the turret*

*base, the handrails for the supporting infantry, the brackets for the external fuel tanks, the well-sloped hull armor, and the wide tracks.*

machine-gun which was ball-mounted on the right-hand side of the glacis plate. The DT machine-gun took its name from V. A. Degtyarev who developed it.

In 1941 the maximum hull armor of the tank was increased to 47mm and that of the turret to 60mm to counter the effect of the German 50mm anti-tank gun which had proved too effective at close quarters. In 1942 an improved cast turret was fitted instead of the welded one and the length of the gun was increased to 41.2 calibers. This model was usually designated the T-34/76B. The T-34/76C which appeared in 1943 had a commander's cupola added to the hexagonal cast turret. Some 76Cs appeared with a welded turret. These changes were accompanied by improvements in the transmission, air filters, range, and production techniques.

Finally, in December 1943 came the most radical change when the T-34 was up-gunned with a 85mm in a three-man turret and became the T-34/85. The modifications required for this were directed by V. V. Krylov. The T34/85 remained in service for more than 20 years. Something in the nature of 50,000 T-34s were built. Many chassis were also used in the SU role.

### Up-Gunned Panzer IV

Faced with the unexpected power of the T-34/76 the Panzer IV at the outset of Barbarossa found itself completely outclassed. As a hurried answer a new gun was designed to replace the short-barrelled 7.5cm. This was the 7.5cm L/43 which was mounted for the first time in the Ausf F, those tanks of this model with the new gun being designated Ausf F2 in the German army and Mark IV Special by the British who came up against them at Alam Halfa and El Alamein in September and October 1942. The Ausf G also carried the L/43 as well as having increased armor. The final Panzer IVs, how-

ever, the Ausf H and Ausf J which appeared in 1943 and 1944, had the L/48 gun. The Ausf H was the most numerous model of the Panzer IV.

But up-gunning was only a stop-gap. What the Germans needed was a new tank to restore the tank superiority they had lost when they encountered the T-34.

### Panther

Work on designing a successor to the Panzer IV began in 1937 but so well did the Panzer IV perform and so many were the changes in ideas and requirements along the way that the project was not pursued with any urgency until the Panzer IV came up against the Russian T-34.

At Guderian's urgent request a commission consisting of representatives of the Army Ordnance, the Armaments Ministry, tank designers and tank builders was sent to the Russian front in November 1941. The commission assessed the three main characteristics of the T-34 which made all existing German tanks technically obsolete. These were: one, the sloped armor which gave optimum shot deflection all round; two, the large road wheels which gave a stable and steady ride; and three, the overhanging gun, a feature which the Germans had previously avoided as being impracticable. Of these it was the sloped armor which was the most revolutionary.

Within a few days the Armaments Ministry had given contracts to Daimler-Benz and MAN to produce designs for a new medium tank in the 30-35 tons class which were to be ready by the spring. The specification was for a vehicle with 60mm of frontal armor and 40mm of side armor, the front and sides being sloped as in the T-34. Maximum speed was to be 55kph.

The designs were ready in April. Daimler-Benz pro-

*Panthers Ausf D on the Russian front in 1944.*

A snow-camouflaged Panzer IV F2 in Russia during the winter of 1942–43. This was the only tank then available to the Wehrmacht capable of defeating the Russian T-34.

The new "Mark IV Specials" – as the British called them – though few in number played an important part in the fierce fire-fight at Alam Halfa. They were armed with the long 7.5 cm KwK 40 L/43.

*Panthers (Ausf. A) of the "Gross Deutschland" Division counter-attacking near Memel, November 1944.*

*General Winter in command. Panzer III with German infantry near Rostov in February 1943.*

posed a tank which was basically a copy of the T-34. MAN proposed a more sophisticated tank but one which was far more conventional by existing German engineering standards. Hitler, who always took a personal interest in ordnance design, preferred the Daimler-Benz proposal although he suggested that the 7.5cm L/48 gun should be changed to the more powerful L/70 weapon. But the "Panther Committee" of the Army Weapons Department preferred the MAN design, and in May 1942 this was accepted. An order for 200 Daimler-Benz vehicles which had been placed because of Hitler's preference was quietly cancelled.

The first pilot model of the MAN tank was completed and tested in September 1942 and the new tank was ordered into immediate production with top priority as PzKpfw V Panther under the ordnance designation SdKfz 171. On Hitler's personal directive at a later stage (27 February 1944) the designation PzKpfw V was dropped and the tank was simply known as the Panther.

The first of the new tanks was turned out by MAN in November 1942. The production target was originally 250 a month, but this was soon increased to 600 a month, a target that was never reached despite the cutting back of aircraft production and the involvement of two other manufacturers (Maschinenfabrik Niedersachsen and Henschel) and scores of subcontractors. In 1943 average production of Panthers was 154 a month and by February 1945 when production tailed off 4,814 Panthers had been built.

The Panther first saw action in the Battle of Kursk in July 1943, but its appearance on the battlefield was not as triumphant as had been hoped. The speed with which it had been produced (a year from inception to the first production vehicle) resulted in a number of teething troubles. Indeed in the early months more Panthers were put out of service by mechanical faults than by Soviet anti-tank guns.

The Panther conformed to the usual layout of German tanks with the driving and transmission compartment forward, the fighting compartment and turret in the center, and the engine compartment at the rear. The driver sat on the left-hand side forward, with the wireless operator, who was also the hull machine-gunner, on the right side forward. The radio equipment was located in the sponson on the operator/gunner's right. Between the driver and the operator was the gearbox with final drive led each side to the front sprockets.

In the turret the gunner sat on the left hand side of the gun, the vehicle commander was at the left rear, and the remaining crew member was the loader who was on the right side of the turret. The gunner fired the gun electrically by a trigger fitted on the elevating handwheel, and the coaxial machine-gun by a foot switch.

The engine, housed in the rear compartment, was a Maybach HL 230 P30 of 700hp at 3,000rpm which gave a maximum speed of 34mph. Like most tank designs the Panther had increased in weight considerably during its development and its fighting weight had grown to 44.75 tons. The thickest armor, 80mm, was on the glacis plate which was sloped at 33° to the horizontal to deflect shells upwards clear of the mantlet. The suspension consisted of eight double interleaved bogie wheels on each side, the wheels being dished disc with solid rubber tires.

The Panther's main armament was a 7.5cm L/70 gun developed by Rheinmetall-Borsig.

There were three basic production models of the Panther which was 29' 1" long, 11' 3" wide, and 9' 9" high. These were Ausfuehrungen D, A, and G — in that order illogical as it seems. The Panther Ausf A was the main type encountered by the Allies in the Normandy fighting, although the Ausf G was also in action there.

The most important derivative from the Panther was the famous Jagdpanther (Hunting Panther) which was a fast powerful tank destroyer. It had an unaltered Panther chassis, but the front and upper side plates were extended upwards to make a well-sloped enclosed superstructure. The gun was an 8.8cm Pak 43/3 L/71

*Tiger company in the Tarnopol area of the Ukraine, spring 1944. Note reserve fuel drums roped to the hull of each tank.*

*A late production Tiger Ausf. E on the Russian front, summer 1944; note the episcope-fitted cupola and "Zimmerit" anti-magnetic plaster ripple coating.*

*"Feifel" air cleaning system at rear, plain cylindrical cupola, and rubber-tyred road wheels are hallmarks of the early production Tiger Ausf. H. These three views show the standard equipment stowage for this vehicle including tow-cables each side, gun cleaning rods each side of turret, tools, and turret bin. The holes just ahead of the vertical front plate are for camouflage support stanchions; the tube on the right side aft is for radio aerial stowage. This vehicle has brackets for "S"-mine dischargers at each corner of the hull top and immediately ahead of the engine decking. (Chamberlain Collection)*

which was mounted to give it a limited traverse of 11° each side. A ball-mounted MG34 was fitted in the right front with the driver in the left front. The complete crew consisted of commander, gunner, two loaders, wireless operator/machine-gunner, and driver.

The building of Jagdpanthers was begun in February 1944 using the Ausf G chassis, and by the end of the war 382 had been completed.

## Tiger

More than a year before the Panther came on to the battlefield the Germans had produced one of the most charismatic tanks of all time. There was something about the Tiger that made it symbolic of armor, both in its appearance and power, and indeed in its name. It was large, menacing, unyielding, and contemptuous of its opposition.

The Tiger had its origins in 1937 when Henschel of Kassel were told to design a 30—33 ton tank code-named DW1 to replace the early Panzer IVs. By 1940 the orignal design had been modified and re-named DW2 — DW standing for *Durchbruchswagen*, breakthrough vehicle. Trials were carried out with a prototype chassis until 1941 when Henschels were given a specification for another vehicle of the same class and weight as the DW2, the new vehicle being identified as VK3001. The order was also given to Henschel's competitors — Porsche, MAN, and Daimler-Benz.

The Henschel version VK3001(H) was a development of the DW2. The superstructure resembled the Panzer IV and the suspension consisted of seven interleaved road wheels and three return rollers each side. It was planned to mount the 7.5cm L/48 gun in this vehicle, but the appearance of the T-34 with its 76mm gun put paid to the VK3001(H). The Porsche version, VK3001(P), incorporated several new design features including gasoline-electric drive and longitudinal torsion bar suspension. Both the MAN and Daimler-Benz versions were also aborted.

*A later production Panther Ausf D which shows the dustbin-type cupola and the vision port and machine-gun port on the glacis.*

Concurrently with the order for VK3001 an additional order was placed for a 36-ton tank designated VK3601. It was Hitler himself who proposed the specification: a powerful high velocity gun, heavy armor, and a maximum speed of at least 25mph. A prototype of this project was built by Henschel, but work on both the VK3001 and VK3601 was stopped when yet another order was received, this time for a 45-ton tank. This VK4501 was to carry a tank version of the famous 8.8cm gun which had proved itself to be such an effective anti-aircraft and anti-tank weapon. With the order came the stipulation that the prototype was to be ready for demonstration to Hitler on his birthday, 20 April 1942.

Because time was short Henschels incorporated the best features of VK3001(H) and VK3601(H) into the new vehicle. Porsche also received the order for a 45-tonner and similarly they too incorporated features from the VK3001(P) into their version.

*The Panther Ausf G, the final production type had several improvements. Notable is the simplified hull shape with a continuous sloping line to the lower sponson edges, the deletion of the driver's vision ports and episcopes and the substitution of a rotating periscope.*

# ORIGINAL PANZER DIVISIONAL SIGNS

1st Panzer

2nd Panzer

3rd Panzer

4th Panzer

5th Panzer

6th Panzer

7th Panzer

8th Panzer

9th Panzer

10th Panzer

## PANZER DIVISIONAL SIGNS FROM LATE 1940

After their victory in France in 1940 the Germans doubled the number of their panzer divisions for the next campaign. Signs of the old divisions were changed and the new signs shown here were introduced. Panzer divisions from 21 onwards were formed after 1940. The Gross Deutschland was officially a panzer grenadier division but with its full tank regiment and armoured reconnaissance unit under command it was actually a panzer division.

1st Panzer

2nd Panzer

3rd Panzer

4th Panzer

6th Panzer

5th Panzer

7th Panzer

8th Panzer

9th Panzer

10th Panzer

11th Panzer

12th Panzer

Gross Deutschland

13th Panzer

14th Panzer

15th Panzer

16th Panzer

17th Panzer

18th Panzer

19th Panzer

20th Panzer

21st Panzer

22nd Panzer

23rd Panzer

24th Panzer

25th Panzer

Afrika Korps

116th Panzer

Afrika Korps
(variation)

1st Panzer
(variation)

4th Panzer (1943)

7th Panzer
(1943–44)

19th Panzer
(1943–44)

23rd Panzer
(variation)

26th Panzer

Panzer Lehr

Kurmark

Feldherrnhalle 2

Hermann Goering

12th Panzer
(variation)

## SS PANZER DIVISIONAL SIGNS

1st SS Panzer
Leibstandarte
Adolf Hitler

2nd SS Panzer
Das Reich

3rd SS Panzer
Totenkopf

5th SS Panzer
Wiking

9th SS Panzer
Hohenstanfen

9th SS Panzer
(variation after Arnhem
1944 – red windmill)

10th SS Panzer
Frundsberg

12th SS Panzer
Hitler Jugend

*Panther Ausf G*

The demonstration duly took place before Hitler at Rastenburg on his birthday. The Henschel design was preferred and production began in August. Originally designated Panzerkampfwagen VI Tiger Ausf H SdKfz 181 this was changed in February 1944 to PzKpfw Tiger Ausf E SdKfz 181. The tank was in production for two years from August 1942 to August 1944 during which time 1,350 were built.

It is interesting to note that the specified weight of 45 tons was considerably exceeded. The Tiger weighed 56 tons. It was 20′ 9″ long, 12′ 3″ wide, 9′ 5″ high. It was powered originally by a Maybach V-12 gasoline engine, the 650hp HL 210 P45 of 21 litres, but it was soon realised that the vehicle was under-powered and from December 1942 the 700hp P45 of 24 litres was substituted. Its main armament was a 8.8cm L/56.1 KwK36 gun, and it had two 7.92mm machine-guns, one coaxial, the other mounted in the right hull front. The Tiger had a crew of five — commander, gunner, loader, driver, hull gunner/radio operator. The hull was divided into four compartments: a forward pair housing the driver and the hull gunner, a central fighting compartment, and a rear engine compartment. The driver sat on the left and steered by means of a steering wheel which acted hydraulically on the tank's controlled differential steering unit. The floor of the fighting compartment was suspended from the turret by three steel tubes and rotated with the turret. The breech mechanism of the 88 reached almost to the inside rear turret wall, dividing the fighting compartment virtually in two.

The Porsche VK4501 design had been ordered into production temporarily as a stand-by and the chassis for 90 vehicles were used for a self-propelled 8.8cm L/71 gun called first the Ferdinand in honor of Dr Ferdinand Porsche and then the Elefant.

When the Tiger appeared on the battlefield in late 1942 in front of Leningrad its baptism of fire was inauspicious because the terrain was unsuitable for tank action and, restricted as the tanks were to single file progress on forest tracks through swamps, they proved easy targets for the Soviet gunners who were covering the tracks. Nevertheless things did not always go against them. Far from it. With their 100mm maximum armor and powerful main armament the Tigers were the most formidable tanks in service in any army at that time.

The Tiger was the first German combat tank to be fitted with over-lapping road wheel suspension. This was adopted to give optimum weight distribution. There were eight independently sprung torsion bar axles on each side. In order to carry all the axles inside the hull envelope it was necessary to stagger them on the floor so that the right hand axles trailed aft and the left hand axles led forward. Though this type of suspension gave a superior ride it also had its drawbacks; one being that the road wheels became packed with mud and snow in the winter; if allowed to freeze this could jam the wheels. The Russians took advantage of this by timing their attacks for dawn when the Tigers were likely to be immobilized.

Tigers were issued to independent battalions which were alloted to other formations as required. Panzer divisions engaged in a major operation would be given a Tiger unit or sub-unit to spearhead its attack with the more maneuverable Panzer IIIs and IVs on the flanks. Later it was decided to include Tigers in the normal organization of a panzer division but the shortage of serviceable Tigers meant that in fact only the seven Waffen SS panzer divisions received them. As Peter Chamberlain has wisely commented, "the fact that there were never sufficient Tigers to go round was probably the greatest comfort that opposing forces could take from their appearance."

In 1944, as well as the seven SS panzer divisions there were 26 army panzer divisions. There was also the Hermann Goering-Panzer Division. The army panzer

*Porsche's Panzerjaeger Tiger, originally called Ferdinand (after Porsche) and then re-named Elefant. It was simply a conversion of the original Porsche Tiger tank design to a self-propelled anti-tank weapon. It fought in Operation Citadel, on other parts of the Eastern front, and then in Italy. This vehicle has the additional protection in front of the gun mantlet which was a retrospective modification made after experience in the field.*

divisions were numbered 1 to 27 inclusive and Gross Deutschland, all formed before the end of 1942, plus the 116th formed in spring 1944 and Panzer Lehr. Of these the 10th, 18th, 22nd, and 27th were destroyed or disbanded (the 18th) in 1943 and not re-formed. The 14th, 15th, 21st, and 24th were destroyed in 1943 but all were re-formed.

On the eve of the battle of Normandy in June 1944 the standard panzer division had two tank battalions (one generally equipped with Panzer IVs, the other with Panthers.) Only one of its three artillery battalions had SP guns, and only one of the four infantry bat-

talions had armored personnel carriers. Tank battalions had four companies, each, in theory, of 22 tanks. In practise it was usually three companies of 17 tanks each: by the end of the war it was 14. Some panzer divisions — especially the SS — were favored and had three tank battalions; some even more — the Gross Deutschland, for example, had four (one of Tigers) and six infantry battalions. Special Panzer Lehr establishment when it became a division late in 1943 was two tank battalions, each of four companies, with a divisional HQ company of Tigers; its infantry battalions had half-tracks, and artillery units had SP guns.

*Ausf H, the penultimate Panzer IV model, had the L/48.75 gun as its main armament, as did Ausf. J, the last model. The cupola lid which had been divided in two in earlier models now became a circular one piece lid. Driving sprocket and idler wheel were changed. Front armor was increased to 80mm. In Ausf. J the power traverse was replaced by a two-speed hand gear to provide room for increased fuel capacity. A new gearbox in later Ausf. H vehicles and in Ausf. J, gave improved cross country performance. Mesh Schürzen instead of plates were sometimes used on Ausf. J vehicles. Weight of Ausf J. was 25 tons, slightly less than Ausf. H. These two models together accounted for about two-thirds of the total number of Panzer IVs produced. In appearance they were very similar. Note rail on side from which Schürzen were suspended.*

*It was at the 1940 maneuvers that the adhoc armored division dominated the scene. On July 10, 1940 the Armored Force was created.*

# V
# 1941—45: Pearl Harbor: Before and After — The USA in the War

The United States ended World War I with a Tank Corps of nearly 16,000 officers and men and a tank building program of 23,000 tanks. This program was never realized. Barely a dozen American-built tanks reached France in 1918, none in time for combat and after the Armistice the large tank orders were cancelled. Even so, deliveries under outstanding contracts gave the Tank Corps 1,163 American-built tanks. These were to be the main equipment of the armored units throughout the 1920s and early 1930s, for only 35 tanks were built from 1920 until 1935 and some of these were re-builds of one another. Indeed, between the two world wars no leading nation made less progress in tank development and production than the United States. By contrast no nation built as many tanks as the United States during World War II. From 1940 until the end of the war in 1945 the U.S. built 28,919 light tanks, 57,027 medium tanks, and 2,330 heavy tanks — a total of 88,276. Altogether, American output of armored combat vehicles, including Amtracs totalled 337,388.

And as well as this enough spare parts were made to have produced half as many more again. The gigantic volume of American output is the outstanding feature of armored combat in World War II.

All that was far in the future in 1920 when the American Tank Corps was disbanded. Henceforward all tank units were to form part of the infantry and were to be known as 'Infantry (Tanks)'. Despite this restriction a Mechanized Force, influenced by the British experiment the previous year, was assembled at Camp Meade, Maryland, for three months in 1928. It was a force of all arms — infantry (tanks), cavalry, field artillery, air corps, engineers, ordnance, chemical warfare services, and the medical corps. The force did not become permanent. General Douglas MacArthur, the incoming Chief of Staff, in 1931 ordered that 'mechanisaltion and motorisation' should be adopted by the whole U.S. Army and should not be confined to a specialised force. The cavalry was instructed to develop combat vehicles which would enhance its usual roles.

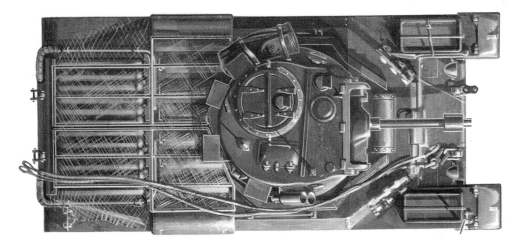

The Australian Matilda Frog was a standard Matilda 4 modified to carry flamethrowing equipment in the turret. It went into action against the Japanese in the assault landings on Borneo in July 1945, operated by the 2/1st Armoured Brigade Reconnaissance Squadron. This tank bears the unit markings and the sign of 4 Australian Armoured Brigade, which was formed specifically for operations in tropical areas. It is painted the dark green that was best for jungle warfare.

Local modifications, which could be of varied design, were fitted to most Matildas for this fighting at close quarters, and two of these are shown; an armoured shield on the hull top to protect the turret ring, and anti-magnetic mine screens over the engine louvres.

0          5'

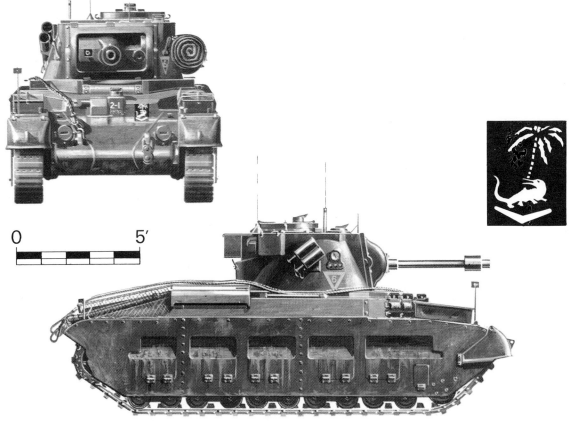

## T-34/76B

This painting was based on a T-34 operating in the Kharkov area in the spring of 1943. It is identifiable as a T-34/76B, introduced in 1942, by the long – 41·2 calibre – 76·2 mm. gun. It has improved hull and cast turret armour. It is a company commander's tank for only these were fitted with radio. It should be noted that all other external features are the same as the short 76 mm. gun 7-34/76A, including the large, one-piece turret hatch. The addition of a commander's cupola in 1943 identified the T-34/76C which also sometimes had a welded turret. The Red Army star insignia and the Guards insignia, a battle honour awarded to elite units and won by many Red Army armoured regiments, were only added to Soviet fighting vehicles on ceremonial occasions. They fought usually devoid of any unit or identification marks except, occasionally, a company number as seen on this specimen.

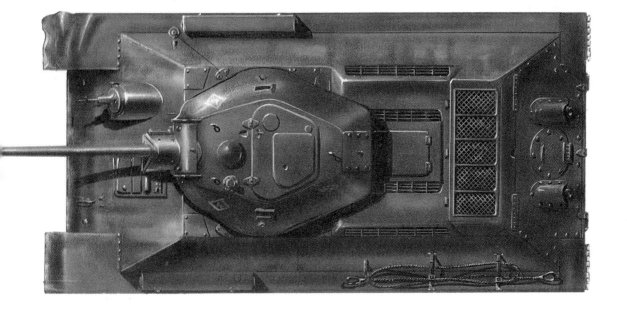

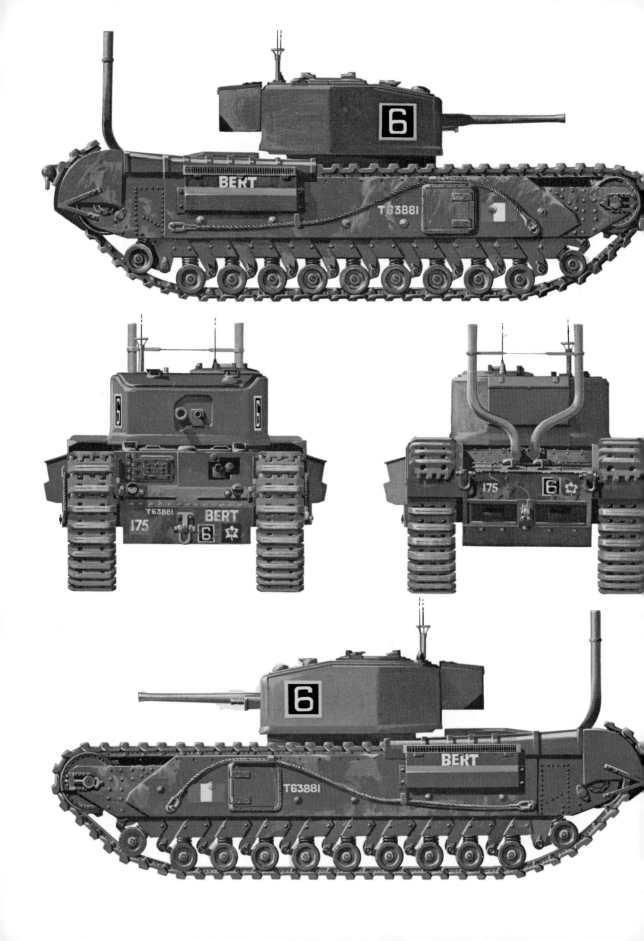

Churchill III of the Calgary Regiment, 1st Canadian Tank Brigade,
equipped with exhaust extension for deep wading, Dieppe, August
19th, 1942.

34 ARMD BDE

0′         5′         10′

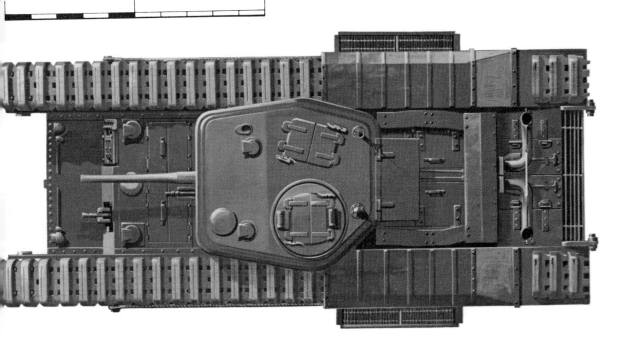

*(Above)* Side view of Type 89B Medium Tank CHIRO with ditching tail.

*(Below)* Side view of Type 1 Medium Tank CHIHE. The CHIHE was the Type 97 Medium Tank CHIHA with modifications including different main armament.

*(Right)* Four views of Type 97 Medium Tank CHIHA.

The tanks are shown in their original "workshop finish" camouflage colours, i.e. before these had faded through weathering and active service

0                                    5ft

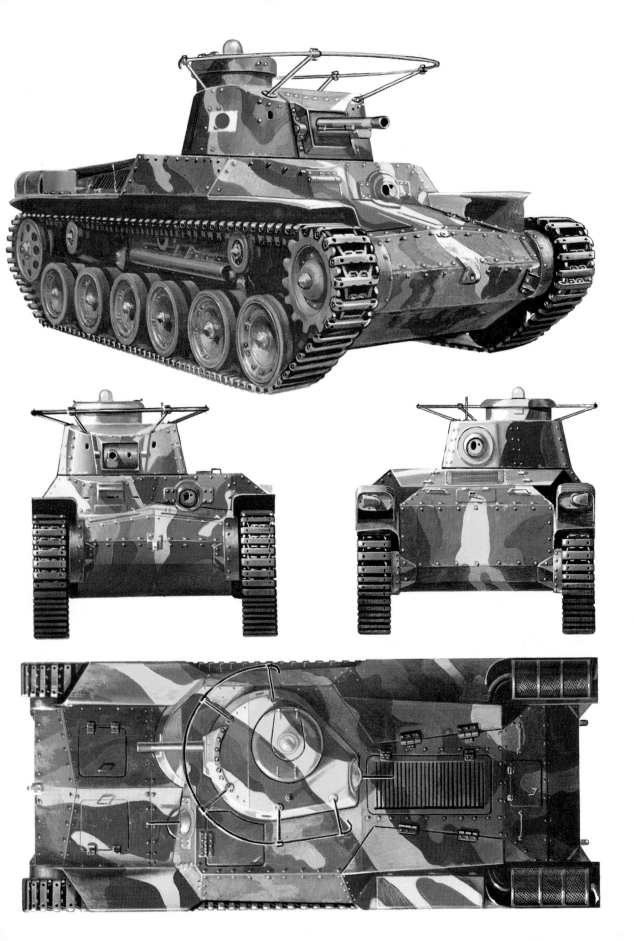

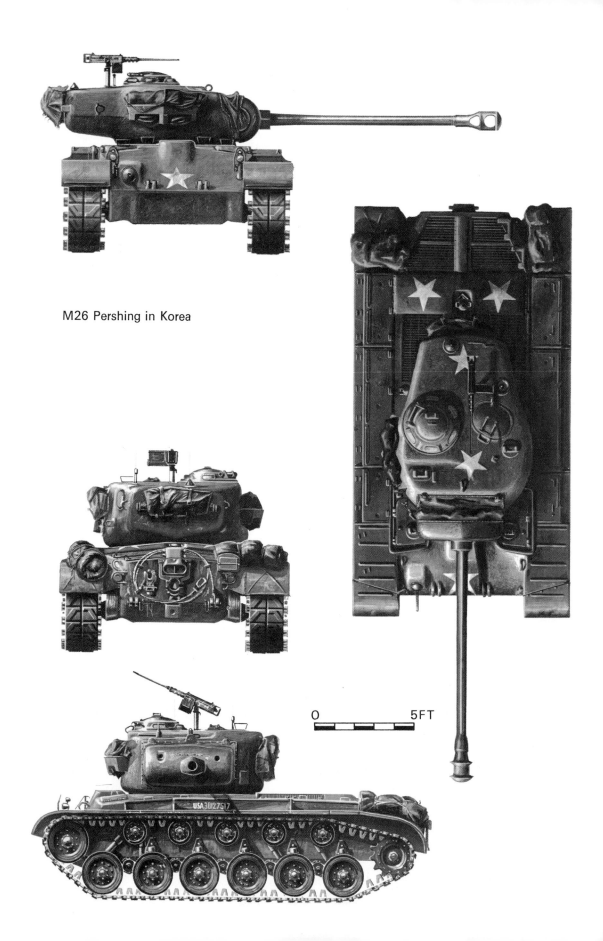

M26 Pershing in Korea

0          5FT

The infantry, on the other hand, was to concentrate on developing tanks which would support the rifleman in the assault. In effect therefore the essence of the Mechanised Force was handed over to the cavalry.

## Medium Tanks

Post-war tank development up to this time was based on a paper written before the abolition of the Tank Corps by one of its officers. It suggested that two types of tanks should be produced: a light tank in the five ton class and a medium tank in the 20 to 30 ton class. The first medium tank was built in 1921. Called the Medium A, or M1921, it weighed 23 tons and was armed with a 6-pounder in the turret and a machine-gun in a cupola. The following year the Medium M1922 was produced. It was similar to the M1921 but was more akin to the British Medium D in its configuration, with its track frames higher in the rear than in the front. The M1922 weighed 25 tons and had a speed of 12mph. Both these tanks were ruled out for further development because of a General Staff directive cutting the maximum weight of a medium tank to 15 tons because of existing engineer bridging material and the limitations imposed by railroad flat cars and highway bridges. A lighter mock-up of the M1921 was made, called the M1924. In 1926 permission was given to build a heavier tank, also similar to the M1921 and weighing 23 tons like the original. This was designated the Medium T1. In 1931 it was re-built with a different engine and improved ventilation and became the Medium T1E1.

By this time (1930) the Ordnance Department had built the Medium T2 which conformed to the 15 ton limit. It was based on the British Medium Mark II and resembled it in general shape and layout. Its armament was a 37mm gun and a machine-gun in the right front plate, and a 47mm and .50 inch machine-gun in the turret. In 1931 the Medium T2 Modified was produced, with a lower hull and without the 37mm gun. A .30 inch machine-gun was added for anti-aircraft fire.

*Medium Tank M2 (and its similar but improved successor the M2A1) were the designs which formed the mechanical basis for the M3 Mediums. Note the numerous machine-guns, the single 37mm. gun in the turret, and the deflector plates for enfilading trenches in line with the rear-firing machine-guns.*

Throughout this period J. Walter Christie was inventing and developing AFVs. The Medium T3 and T4 were both Christie vehicles. Three Medium T3 tanks were delivered to the infantry and four to the cavalry. Because only the infantry were allowed to have tanks the cavalry's vehicles were called combat cars, the cavalry's Medium T3 becoming Combat Car T1 and the thinner armored Medium T4 becoming the Combat Car T4.

## Light Tanks

In 1924 the infantry decided that they only wanted medium tanks, but two years later they completely reversed this policy and at the very time the Medium T1 was being produced they decided that henceforth they wanted only light tanks. With the collaboration of the Society of Automobile Engineers the T1 Light tank series was initiated.

*The 23-ton medium tank of 1926 was developed from the earlier Medium A or M1921 and the Medium M1922. It was designated Medium T1. It appeared at a time when the Infantry, having in 1924 decided that it wanted only medium tanks, reversed that decision and now opted for light tanks only. Although the Infantry were the sole users of tanks, medium tank development nevertheless continued.*

*The M2A4 saw limited combat service. This U.S. Marine Corps vehicle moves forward into the jungle at Guadalcanal Island, Solomons, in September 1942. It belongs to the same battalion as the M3 light tank shown as a colour illustration.*

The T1 Light tank was produced in 1927. Its engine was at the front, its bevel-fronted cylindrical turret at the rear. It was armed with a short 37mm gun and a co-axial machine-gun in the turret. Over the next few years modifications were made to the original, the main change coming with the T1E4 which had its hull reversed with the engine in the rear.

The purpose of the T1 Light tank was to support the rifleman in the attack, but in 1932 General MacArthur brushed aside this concept of the tank that could only move at the speed of the infantry it was accompanying.

What was needed, he said, was a tank with 'a high degree of tactical mobility'. Light tank development immediately took a new turn. To meet the MacArthur requirements the T2 Light appeared, sacrificing armor protection for high speed and small caliber guns. For reasons of economy — a paramount factor — the design was adaptable for both the infantry and the cavalry.

The T2 was capable of 35mph. In its T2E1 version it had volute spring suspension instead of the double leaf spring articulated bogie type. The T2E2 version

*A Combat Car M1 of the U.S. 1st Cavalry Regt, 7th Cavalry Brigade, seen at high speed during 1939 manoeuvres.*

had the same suspension as the T2E1 but differed from it in having twin turrets side by side which severely limited their traverse. The T2E1 had a single turret. Similar to T2E1 was the T5E2 Combat Car which was developed for the cavalry.

## Production

In 1938 there was a change in the 1931 policy directive. In future mechanization would no longer be developed by all arms but only by the infantry and cavalry. The armor enthusiasts, given their head, now began to press ever more loudly for the United States Army to have armored divisions. With so little money available for tanks since 1918 the General Staff's policy had been to devote such funds as it had to development rather than to quantity production. This proved to be a policy with infinite benefits. Several vehicle components developed during these frugal years were the mainstays of tank design in World War II — volute spring suspension and air-cooled radial aricraft-type engines, to name only two.

By 1938, however, the years of development were cautiously giving way to the years of production. The Medium T4 was the first tank to be built in quantity — only 16 it is true — as opposed to the previous vehicles that had been only prototypes or a series of prototypes. In 1938 the pilot of the Medium T5 was completed. With eight machine-guns it was a moving armory for infantry support — as conceived at that period. A modified T5 was standardised as the M2 Medium in 1939 and 18 were built.

*The first M3 completed was built by American Locomotive Co. and was tested at Aberdeen Proving Ground in April 1941 where it is here seen.*

In the light tank class the T2E2 was standardized as the M2A2 Light tank and the T5E2 Combat Car was standardized as the Combat Car M1. About 170 M2A2 Light tanks and M1 Combat Cars were built. Both models were improved and re-designated M2A3 Light tank and M2 Combat Car respectively. Some 50 were built, production being completed by early 1939.

The M2A3 was further improved. Instead of the twin turrets a small single riveted manually traversed turret was installed with a 37mm gun and a co-axial .30 machine-gun. The new tank, designated M2A4, had

*Early M3s in U.S. Army service take part in exercises in October 1941. Note that they lack the 75mm gun, still in short supply at this period. Troops are still wearing 1918 type steel helmets.*

*Grant squadron of the Royal Tank Regiment in the Desert, May 1942, when this tank first went into action in the Gazala battle.*

four other .30 machine-guns: one in the bow, two in fixed forward-firing mounts (one in each side sponson), and one on a pintle at the turret rear for AA fire. The tank's trials were completed in September 1939 as Germany attacked Poland with the result that instead of being just another development vehicle the M2A4 became the first American mass-produced tank, albeit this production was on a minor scale compared with the output that was to come later.

When the Germans launched their *Blitzkrieg* against France and the Low Countries in May 1940 the American reaction was an urgent acceleration of the re-armament program. At that time the United States had only a few hundred tanks, most of them museum pieces of World War I vintage that had been laid up since the early 1930s. Apart from these and the handful of proto-types there were the Combat Cars and early M2A2 and M2A3 Light tanks and the few Medium T4s. There were only 28 tanks which could be called new — 18 M2 Mediums and the first 10 M2A4 Lights.

On June 30 a National Munitions Program was in-troduced, covering all aspects of war equipment including the creation of new arsenals to produce tanks on a mas-sive scale. In particular the need for medium tanks armed with guns of at least 75mm caliber had been made vital by the German Panzer IV. Tanks like the M2 and M2A1 Mediums with their 37mm guns had been tactically outmoded almost overnight.

## M3 Medium — Lee/Grant

On July 10 the Armored Force was created as a separate branch of the U.S. Army, and on the 15th the I Armor-ed Corps consisting of the 1st and 2nd Armored Divisions was activated. The tank that resulted from the need to match the Panzer IV was the M3 Medium, developed from the experimental work that had already been done on mounting a 75mm gun in the barbette of the T5E2 Medium. It was not immediately possible to mount a gun of this caliber in the turret of the tank be-cause no turret of sufficient size had ever previously been built in the U.S. and it would take time to over-come the problems involved. Consequently the M3

Medium had its 75mm gun mounted in the right of the hull and the rangefinder turret of the T5E2 was offset to the left and a 37mm gun mounted in it.

Thus the M3 Medium came into being as an interim tank while work continued on designing a medium tank with a 75mm gun in a fully traversing turret. This be-came the M4 Medium, better known as the Sherman, the most numerous tank built by the USA.

The M3 was mainly built in Chrysler's Detroit Tank Arsenal which was constructed from scratch starting in September 1940, and by two locomotive firms. The 75mm gun, the design for which was based on the famous French 75, was carried out by the Watervliet Arsenal. The first version, designated M2, had a barrel 84 inches long and a muzzle velocity of 1,800fps. The later model, the M3, had a 110 inch barrel and a muzzle velocity of 2,300fps. Both the 75 and 37 guns in the M3 Medium had gyro-stabilisers fitted. This was a revolutionary innovation in a tank although the prin-ciple had long been used in naval gunnery. It maintained the gun at any given elevation irrespective of the pitch-ing of the vehicle as it moved across country thus enabling the gunner to fire on the move with accuracy.

The pilot models of the M3 Medium were ready early in April 1941 and the M3 first entered U.S. Army ser-vice in late summer 1941. The last M3s left the production lines in December 1942. The M3 was hardly used in combat by the U.S. Army, being mainly a train-ing tank, but it was a valuable part of the fighting strength of the British and Australian armies.

In June 1940 a British Mission arrived in the U.S. to arrange contracts with American firms to build tanks for Britain. The Mission was told that it must accept American designs or nothing because the situation would not permit the dispersion of effort which special designs would entail. The British took the only two types in the pipeline — the M3 Medium and the M3 Light (see below). Various modifications were made in the M3 Medium for British use. The turret was changed to accommodate the wireless equipment which British practise installed in the turret rather than in the hull as in American and German tanks. The machine-gun cupola was also eliminated. The British version was called the Grant (after the General) and first saw action in the Gazala battle in North Africa in May 1942. For the first time the British had a high velocity gun which could match the best German guns and which could give indirect support fire with HE, a facility lacking in all previous tanks in British service. "The advent of the new American tank had torn great holes in our ranks," wrote Rommel ruefully in his journal. "Our entire force now stood in heavy and destructive combat with a superior enemy."

The British also received the standard M3 Medium which they called the Lee. Grants and Lees, together with Shermans which were just arriving, were the preponderant tanks in the Second Battle of Alamein in October 1942. For five months the M3 Medium played a crucial part in the Western Desert fighting. The other theatre in which the tank had a splendid career was Burma. Five regiments were equipped with Lees, including 146 Regiment RAC which got its revenge for the Donbaik affair when it helped to oust the Japanese from the Arakan from January to April 1945. The other regiments which fought in Lees were 149 and 150 Regiments RAC, 25th Dragoons, and the Carabiniers. The attack by 150 Regiment on Magwe on 19 April 1945 was the only occasion during the war when a complete regiment of Lees made a regimental attack; in the Western Desert there was always one squadron of Stuarts or two squadrons of Crusaders in a Lee regiment.

The Carabiniers arrived at Imphal in December 1943 and first went into action there in March 1944. From then until their arrival in Rangoon on 28 May 1945 they fought their way for 1,100 miles in their Lees "with battles all the way and over ground at which," says the regimental history, "the imagination boggles." Included in this journey, after the capture of Tiddim, was the

*General Montgomery, 8th Army Commander, observing battle operations from his temporary command tank, a Grant of the Staffordshire Yeomanry, in the late autumn of 1942.*

ascent of Kennedy Peak by tanks of C Squadron. At nearly 9,000 feet Kennedy Peak is the highest point in the Chin hills, and was the highest ever reached by tanks up to that time. Since then the Battle of Zotila was fought by tanks at 12,000 feet.

Lee/Grants were also used by the Canadians and the Australians though not in action. Indeed at the end of the war in 1945 the Grant was the most numerous tank in Australian service.

The chassis of the M3 Medium was essentially similar to that of the M2 and the M2A1. Suspension consisted of three vertical volute bogies on each side with a rear idler and front sprocket. The Wright Continental R975 9-cylinder air cooled radial engine was at the rear with fuel tanks flanking the engine compartment. The driver sat at the left front of the vehicle with the gearbox be-

*A brand new M3 test fires its guns on the testing-ground which was built adjacent to Detroit Arsenal.*

*Lees and Shermans in British service in a desert leaguer at the time of the Second Battle of Alamein, October 1942.*

side him. He also operated twin machine-guns in the nose. Armor was 2 inches (50mm) thick on the upper hull front and turret and 1½ inches thick on the sides and lower hull front. There was a .30 inch coaxial machine-gun with the 37mm gun in the turret. There was a further .30 inch machine-gun in the cupola.

While the 75mm gun was the tank's great strength it was also a weakness in tactical terms because it had only a limited traverse of 15 degrees on each side and to use it against an outflanking enemy could only be achieved by moving the entire vehicle. Furthermore the gun was set low with the result that the vehicle's high silhouette had to be dangerously exposed before the 75 could be brought into action.

The M3 Medium had a crew of six. It weighed 30 tons

and was 18′ 6″ long, 8′ 11″ wide, and 10′ 3″ high. Its top speed was 26mph. Several changes were made in the design of the M3 series during its production life. Some resulted from combat or user experience while others were production expedients. A particular problem with all American tank production in the 1939—45 period was the constant shortage of suitable engines. The quest for suitable alternative power plants partly led to some of the model changes which followed. The production series for M3 Medium tanks is summarized in chronological order:

*M3:* Original production type as designed with Wright R975 (Whirlwind) engine and all-riveted construction. Built by American Loco (April 1941—August 1942, 385 vehicles), Baldwin (April 1941—March 1942, 295 veh-

*Grant tanks of the 1st Australian Armoured Division in Australia, 1942. The Grant was the most numerous type of tank in Australian service.*

icles), Detroit Tank Arsenal (April 1941— August 1942, 3,243 vehicles), Pressed Steel (July 1941—July 1942, 501 vehicles), Pullman (August 1941—July 1942, 500 vehicles).

*M3 (Diesel):* This was a variation on the standard M3 but with a Guiberson diesel motor replacing the Wright gasoline unit to overcome engine shortages. British designation for the M3 was Lee Mk. I.

*M3A1:* Identical mechanically to the M3, this version differed in having a cast hull. Built by American Loco (February—August 1942, 300 vehicles), this firm having casting facilities for this type of hull.

*M3A1 (Diesel):* As for M3AI but with Guiberson diesel motor. British designation for the M3AI was Lee Mk. II.

*M3A2:* This was similar to the M3 but had a welded instead of a riveted hull. Built by Baldwin (January— February 1942). Only 12 of these were built because the adoption of a new engine led to a designation change.

*M3A3:* This was simply the all-welded M3A2 fitted with twin General Motors 6—71 diesel motors. Built by Baldwin (March—December 1942, 322 vehicles). British designation for the M3A2 was Lee Mk. III and for the M3A3 was Lee Mk. IV. Lee Mk. V was the designation given to a M3A3 re-engined with the Wright R975 unit.

*M3A4:* This was similar to the original M3 but had the Chrysler A-57 Multibank engine replacing the Wright engine. The Chrysler A-57 was a makeshift power unit made up of five automobile engines on a common crankshaft, specially developed for tanks at Detroit Arsenal. The M3A4 was built at Detroit only (June— August 1942, 109 vehicles). The chassis on this model was lengthened slightly to take the bulkier engine. British designation for M3A4 was Lee Mk. VI.

*M3A5:* This was the same as the M3A3 but had a riveted instead of a welded hull. It was built by Baldwin (January—November 1942, 591 vehicles). British designation for this model was Grant Mk. II. The original Grant — the basic M3 with the British type turret — then took the designation Grant Mk. I.

## M4 Medium — Sherman

As soon as the M3 Medium's design had been completed in March 1941 the Ordnance Department began work on its replacement to produce a tank with a 75mm gun in the turret. Of five provisional schemes submitted to it in April the Armored Force selected the simplest for development. Designated Medium Tank T6 this was standardized as the M4 Medium in October 1941.

The M4, known to the British as the Sherman, was built in eleven different plants and hundreds of subcontractors were involved in the supply of components. As originally designed the tank had the same engine and chassis as its predecessors, the M2A1 and the M3. The Continental R975 engine was a very efficient unit which stemmed from the period when it was cheaper to use an existing aero engine than to develop a new

*The Ford-engined M4A3 became the favored U.S. Army production model. This shows a typical 1943 production vehicle with M34A1 Gun Mount, cast nose, gun clamp, and steel tracks.*

Sherman "Firefly". The British re-armed many Shermans, mainly Mark I(M4), Mark II(M4A1), Mark III(M4A2), and Mark V(M4A4), with the 17-pdr. gun to produce the most effective tank in Allied use when France was invaded in 1944. Shown here is a Mark IC (C = 17 pdr. gun). Popular name for the conversion was "Firefly".

"Jumbo" heavy assault tanks (M4A3E2) in Aachen, October 18, 1944.

design specifically for tanks. However the huge rearmament scheme of 1940—42 soon made it apparent that this source of engines would be insufficient to meet demand especially as increased aircraft production was accelerating the need for the same engine in the aircraft industry. The need for alternative engines was already present when the M3 went into production and a few Guiberson T1400 diesels were used to alleviate the supply problem, but these were not used in the M4. Other types were used however and these gave rise to the different models in the M4 series.

Design improvements were also made during the production run of the series which continued from early 1942 right through to the war's end in 1945 and resulted in a total of 53,362 Shermans being built. The quest for more powerful armament was met by the 76mm (3-inch) high velocity gun mounted in a new turret which was designed for the T23, a tank which was intended to succeed the M4 but which was never standardized. With the new turret came "wet stowage" for ammunition to reduce fire hazards. The new racks had an outer "hollow" casing containing a mixture of water and glycerine. Some M4s had the 105mm howitzer as their main armament to provide close support tanks for HQ

companies of medium tank battalions.

Finally in the list of design improvements there was the introduction of horizontal volute spring suspension in place of the vertical volute type to give improved cross-country performance and simpler maintenance. HVSS was fitted from late 1944 onwards and Shermans so fitted were nicknamed "Easy Eights" from the E8 designation applied to the vehicles which carried the trial installation. British Shermans with HVSS had the extra suffix Y added to their designation.

The M4 series models were:

*M4:* This was the original design with Continental engine but with the simplified all-welded hull instead of the cast hull initially devised. It was actually the third type to go into production.

Total production was 8,389, of which 6,748 with 75mm gun and 1,641 with 105mm howitzer.

British designation for the M4 was Sherman I. For those with the 105mm the suffix B was added, i.e. Sherman IB. A late production M4 built at Detroit with combination cast/rolled hull front was designated Sherman Hybrid I.

*M4A1:* Original design based closely on the T6 prototype with cast hull and Continental engine, it was the first type in production.

Total production was 9,677, of which 6,281 with 75mm gun and 3,396 with 76mm gun.

British designation for the M4A1 was Sherman II. For those with the 76mm gun the suffix A was added, i.e. Sherman IIA.

*M4A2:* This was a vehicle with a welded hull but utilising the General Motors 6046 diesel engine. This power unit had been produced from January 1941 for the M3A3 medium tank and was adapted for the M4 immediately production was authorised. The unit consisted of two G.M. truck engines, one each side of the engine compartment, each geared to a common prop shaft. The M4A2 was the second type actually in production, early models following closely after the first M4A1s. The M4A2 was the major type supplied under Lend-Lease to the Russians. Other major users were the British and the U.S. Marines. Few, if any, M4A2s were used by the U.S. Army.

Total production was 11,283, of which 8,053 with 75mm gun and 3,230 with 76mm gun.

British dsignation for the M4A2 was Sherman III. For those with the 76mm gun the suffix A was added, i.e. Sherman IIIA.

*M4A3:* A model with welded hull but utilising the Ford GAA engine, a V-8 unit which was specially developed as a tank engine to replace the Continental. It was authorised for production in January 1942, being developed by Ford on behalf of the Ordnance Department. It subsequently became the new standard tank engine and the M4A3 became the most important model in U.S. service together with the M4 and M4A1. Other types, with extemporised engines, were thereafter mainly allocated to Lend-Lease supplies. Relatively few M4A3s were supplied to other nations.

Total production was 11,424, of which 5,015 with 75mm gun, 3,370 with 76mm gun, and 3,039 with 105mm howitzer.

British designation for the M4A3 was Sherman IV. For those with the 76mm gun the suffix A was added, i.e. Sherman IVA, and for the few, if any, received with the 105mm the suffix B, i.e. Sherman IVB.

*M4A3E2:* The 5,015 M4A3s with 75mm gun included 254 M4A3E2s. The M4A3E2 was an assault tank (nicknamed "Jumbo") built for the close support of infantry in the Normandy campaign. Additional armour was welded to the frontal surfaces to increase the thickness to 4 inches and a new turret was designed with 6 inches of frontal armour; additional rolled plate was also added to the hull top. Weight of the tank was 42 tons compared with an ordinary M4A3's 31—34 tons. Some M4A3E2s were re-armed with a 76mm gun in the field. The 254 M4A3E2s were produced at the Grand Blanc Tank Arsenal in May and June 1944.

*M4A4:* Another extemporised engine was used in this model, this time developed by Chrysler. It featured five 6-cylinder engines on a common shaft. It was first used in the M3A4 built at Detroit Arsenal, and was continued in use in the M4A4. Due to the size of this engine it was necessary to lengthen the rear of the hull and re-space the bogies accordingly. This was the most distinguishing feature of this model. The Chrysler Multibank engine was considered complicated by the Ordnance Department and the M4A4 was the first model to be phased out of production in September 1943. The M4A4 was a major type supplied to the British.

Total production was 7,499, all with 75mm guns.

British designation for the M4A4 was Sherman V.

*M4A5:* There was no M4A5 as such; this designation was used by the U.S. Ordnance Department as a "paper" designation for the Ram, built and developed in Canada.

*M4A6:* As a proposed replacement for the earlier

*Extensive application of spare track shoes was another way of improving the Sherman's protection. This vehicle is crossing the Orne near Caen in August 1944.*

interim engines the Ordnance Department selected the Caterpillar D-200A diesel motor after a series of competitive trials. Under the Ordnance designation RD-1820, this was used to replace the Chrysler engine in the M4A4, the resulting new model becoming the M4A6. However, at the end of 1943 it was decided to standardise on the Ford and Continental engined models only, and M4A6 production came to a premature end. Like the M4A4, the M4A6 had a lengthened rear hull to accommodate the engine, and wider spaced bogies.

Total production was 75, all with 75mm guns.

British designation for the M4A6 was Sherman VII.

*U.S. Marines on Iwo Jima, March 1945. In the foreground late production M4A3s (75mm) wet stowage, and M32 Tank Recovery Vehicle.*

*Convertible Combat Car T7 of 1938 was the last of the Christie type vehicles built in the United States.*

*M4 A1s and infantry moving in to mop up Japanese snipers after the U.S. landing at Hollandia, northern New Guinea, on April 22, 1944.*

*"Hell on Wheels": M4s of the U.S. 2nd Armored Division in the Break-Out between St. Lo and Lessay, Normandy, July 26, 1944. These are re-worked and re-manufactured M4s with applique armor.*

*Cutaway view of an early production M4 A2 showing GMC diesel engines, drive shaft, and gearbox forward. Note ready-use ammunition in turret cage. Gyro-stabiliser is seen immediately below the trunnions and mantlet.*

*Though little publicised by the Russians, several thousand Shermans (M4A2) were delivered to the Soviet Army on Lease-Lend in 1942. Here cavalry pass new Russian Shermans near Kharkov. Note typical Soviet features including the log for unditching, and the extra fuel tanks. Front vehicle has all-steel tracks.*

**Sherman Firefly:** About 600 British Shermans were adapted to take the British high velocity 17 pounder gun as the main armament. These were ready in time for the Normandy campaign and played a vital part against the Panthers and Tigers. Initially, until the supply of 17 pounders improved, there was one of these up-gunned tanks per troop. When armed with the 17 pounder the tank was called the Sherman Firefly. Nearly all marks of Sherman were used as Fireflies, but the most numerous was the Sherman V. When fitted with a 17 pounder the suffix C was added, i.e. Sherman IC, IIC, IIIC, IVC, VC.

Although there were all these different models of the Sherman, the basic vehicle was essentially the same whoever the manufacturer was. Only the engines and minor details varied between models.

All M4 series medium tanks (M4, M4A1, M4A2, M4A3, M4A4, M4A6) were of the same general design and size, and carried the same armament (with the variation between 75mm, 76mm and 105mm detailed earlier). All had identical transmissions, volute spring suspensions (vertical or horizontal), and shoe tracks (steel or rubber). Other identical units were the turret and turret platform, gyro-stabilizer, combination turret

*Across the Adige with umbrella. Sherman of 4th New Zealand Armoured Brigade crossing the last river obstacle in the Italian campaign by pontoon ferry, April 1945.*

*Canadian Shermans attacking towards Falaise, Normandy, August 1944. The nearest tanks are Fireflies.*

*Sherman and one of its opponents. On the left a Tiger captured by the 2nd New Zealand Division near Florence, Italy in July 1944, dwarfs a Sherman of the New Zealanders.*

gun mount and bow gun (.30 inch) mount.

The tank crew consisted of five men. The driver sat at the left bow of the tank, to the left of the transmission. The assistant driver's position was in the right bow, to the right of the transmission and directly behind the bow machine-gun. The tank commander was stationed at the rear of the turret, just to the right of the main gun guard. The gunner's station was almost directly in front of the commander. The loader's station was to the left of the main gun.

For each of the five crew stations there was a periscope, all except the gunner's mounted so that they could be rotated for observation in any direction and tilted to raise or lower the line of vision. The gunner's periscope was connected to the gun mount by linkage that kept the line of vision in constant alignment with the gun as the gun was elevated or depressed. This peri-

*Sherman Crab with flails for minesweeping coming ashore on Walcheren Island, 1 November, 1944.*

97

*Sherman of Probyn's Horse, 255th Indian Tank Brigade in Burma, 1945.*

scope was fitted with a telescope sight so mounted that it could be moved independently of the periscope and the gun for gun-laying.

For the driver and assistant driver, direct vision was provided by horizontal slots in the hull front plate. The slots were fitted with heavy protective covers. In later vehicles, however, these slots were deleted.

A periscope in a revolving mount in the turret hatch was provided for the use of the tank commander when the hatch was closed. All late production vehicles of the 1944—45 period, however, had a new vision cupola with six episcopes which offered a great improvement over the original arrangement.

Access to the tank was provided by two hatches in the bow and a revolving hatch in the turret. For use in an emergency, a quick-opening escape hatch was provided in the tank floor behind the assistant driver.

All models had a radio and an interphone system for crew communication. The radio and interphone were shock-mounted on a common base located on a shelf in the turret bulge.

The turret carried a combination mount for a 75mm gun and a .30 inch machine-gun. The turret platform, or basket, rotated with the turret, which could be traversed through 360 degrees either by hand cranks or by electric-hydraulic drive.

The combination gun mount allowed the gun to be elevated 25 degrees above the horizontal and depressed 10 degrees.

The turret guns could be manually elevated or depressed by operating the elevating handwheel. When the gyro-stabilizer was in operation, the gun was elevated by hydraulic power controlled by the elevating handwheel, and the gyro-stabilizer automatically held the gun steady at any quadrant angle of elevation at which it had been laid, while the tank was in motion.

The two turret guns were fired electrically by means of the firing buttons (foot-operated switches) to the left of the gunner.

The vehicle was steered by means of levers, which operated steering brakes in the differential housing. Braking was effected by pulling back both steering brakes at once.

A typical Sherman, the M4A3, was 19′ 9″ long, 8′ 9″ wide, 9′ 3″ high. Armor was from 15mm minimum to 100mm maximum. Top speed was 30mph and range was 130 miles.

The importance of the Sherman to the Western Allied armored forces cannot be exaggerated. Shermans equipped all the medium tank battalions and medium tank companies in the 16 armored divisions of the U.S. army and the non-divisional medium tank battalions and medium tank companies. It was also the most widely used tank in the British and Commonwealth armies from 1943 until the end of the war. Several thousand were sent to the Russians in 1942, as indeed were many thousand other American and British tanks during the course of the war.

A justified encomium for the Sherman has been written by Chamberlain and Ellis. "By 1944 the Sherman had reached the peak of its development and in its final form with HVSS and the 76mm gun, it proved equal to the *Blitzkreig* role for which it was mainly used. Ironically the U.S. armored divisions in N.W. Europe at this time were using those tactics against the German army which had demonstrated their effectiveness four years earlier. This time the German army was on the defensive and had developed armor — such as the Tigers, Panthers and the various heavy assault guns — more suitable for a defensive war than the lighter Panzers which spearheaded the armored battles of 1939—42. No Sherman could — on paper — stand up to a Tiger or Panther, but the U.S. armies in N.W. Europe had the priceless advantage of supporting air power, adequate reserves, superb logistics, and overwhelming superiority of numbers. In these conditions the tank became a component of a coordinated attack scheme. The main requirement was for mobility, reliability, and adequate armament, and the M4A3 Sherman 76mm had all these qualities. In vast outflanking movements which avoided the heaviest enemy armor — leaving it to be dealt with by tank destroyers and aircraft — the Sherman was used spectacularly as an instrument of advance and exploitation. Exceptional distances like the 151 miles covered in 36 hours by a battalion of the 4th Armored Division in Patton's Third Army during the Battle of the Bulge serve as an indication of the M4's true value as a fighting weapon."

## M3—M5 Light — Stuart

The first production M2A4 Light tank was delivered by its builders, American Car and Foundry Company, in April 1940, and a total of 375 were built. An im-

*The Battle of the Bulge. A Sherman of 774th Battalion, 3rd U.S. Army, passes a knocked out German Panther in the forest near Bovigny, Belgium, January 17, 1945.*

proved version was standardized on July 5, 1940 as the M3 Light tank. In this the armor thickness was increased, the large vision slits in the turret sides were eliminated, and a trailing idler was substituted for a fixed idler so lengthening ground contact and improving stability. Engine covers were thickened for increased protection against air attack and the hull was extended to the rear to cover the previously exposed exhaust pipes and silencers.

Production of the M3 by the American Car and Foundry Co followed on production of the M2A4 without a gap, the first tank leaving the line in March

1941. The M2A4 should not be forgotten as a fighting tank. It formed the major part of the Armored Force's tank strength in 1940—41 and saw combat in the Pacific in 1942, for example on Guadalcanal.

The M2—M3 series had many faults compared with the German tanks they were likely to have to face. Fundamentally they were too high and too narrow with consequent disadvantages in the size of gun that could be mounted and the width of track which gave inadequate ground pressure. A number of modifications, including a gyro-stabiliser for the 37mm gun, were made to the M3 during the course of the production run

*Flame-throwing Sherman of 713 Tank Battalion in action on Okinawa, June 1945.*

*Sherman of the 13/18th Royal Hussars, 8th British Armoured Brigade, beside the River Waal, Holland, October 1944.*

which totalled 5,811 vehicles between March 1941 and August 1942.

In April 1942 an improved model, the M3A1, went into production. This had a turret basket and power traverse as well as the gyro-stabiliser. The cupola was removed to lower the height and the two sponson-mounted .30 inch machine-guns were eliminated in order to provide more ammunition space. The M3A1 was standardized in August 1942, and 4,621 were built from April 1942 to January 1943.

The final and much refined variant of the M3 series was the M3A3 which had an all-welded hull with angled sides and no separate sponsons and with the radio moved from the fighting compartment to a bulge added in the rear of the turret. Production of the M3A3 was started in December 1942 and 3,427 were built before M3 series production ceased in favour of a new model, the M5A1. Incidentally there was no M3A2.

In order to overcome the shortage of engines Cadillac Division of General Motors suggested that two standard V-8 Cadillac engines be ganged together side by side to provide the necessary power and that the newly-developed Cadillac Hydra-matic automatic transmission be used in conjunction with the twin engines. The Ordnance Department was doubtful but Cadillac

*Sherman of the Guards Armoured Division at the liberation of Brussels, September 3–4, 1944.*

proved their point by driving a converted M3 500 miles to the Ordnance Department's test ground at Aberdeen, Maryland without any trouble on the way.

The modified tank (M3E2) was standardized as the M4 Light tank — later changed to M5 to avoid possible confusion with the M4 Medium which was in full production at the time. With its automatic transmission the M5 Light broke new ground for a tank. The first M5s were completed at the end of March 1942: total production was 2,074. In December 1942 an improved model, the M5A1, replaced it; 6,810 M5A1s were built. Production ceased in June 1944 by which time the M24 Light had begun to appear.

Weighing 12.2 tons the M3 was 14′ 10″ long, 7′ 4″ wide, 8′ 3″ high, with either a 7-cylinder Continental radial or a 9-cylinder Guiberson radial diesel engine. The M5 weighed 14.7 tons, was 14′ 3″ long, 7′ 4″ wide, 7′ 6″ high, and, as mentioned above had twin Cadillac V-8 engines. The range of the M3 was 70 miles, of the M5 100 miles. The maximum road speed of both was 36mph.

The M3—M5 series' layout followed conventional U.S. tank practise with a rear engine, drive to front sprockets, and controlled differential steering. Gears and drive were in the nose with the driver on the left and the assistant driver/hull gunner on the right of the gearbox. With easy engine access, ample power (the power to weight ratio was 18 for the M3 and 15 for the M5), sturdy rubber tracks, and tough easily replaceable volute bogies they were among the most reliable tanks ever produced. Their sturdiness was indeed remarkable. In Burma during the retreat in 1942 Stuarts of the 2nd Royal Tanks covered about 2,400 miles in eleven weeks during which very little time could be spent on maintenance.

It was in fact the British who first took the M3 into action. In August 1941 the 8th King's Royal Irish Hussars were equipped with M3s that arrived in Egypt with the first Lease-Lend shipment the previous month. Other units in the 4th Armoured Brigade were also equipped with Stuarts or Honeys as the British called them. They fought their first battle at Sidi Rezegh on 19 November and suffered severely against the 50mm Panzer IIIs and 75mm Panzer IVs.

As well as being used by the Commonwealth armies in the Middle East, New Guinea, Iraq, Italy and North-West Europe, Stuarts returned to the fight in Burma. But it was in the U.S. army that the M3—M5s were employed in the greatest numbers. They equipped all the light tank companies and light tank battalions of the armored formations until they began to be replaced gradually by M24 Chaffee Light tanks towards the end of the war.

## M22 Light — Locust

Another American light tank was the M22. Weighing 7.4 tons, with a crew of three and armed with a 37mm gun and a coaxial .30 inch Browning, the M22 was designed as an airborne tank, but was never used in action by the U.S. forces. The tank was built by Marmon-Herrington. In appearance it was rather like a miniature Sherman, 12′ 11″ long, 7′ 4″ wide, 5′ 4″ high. Suspension was two bogie assemblies of two wheels each per side using volute springs with two support rollers. The assembly was strengthened by means of a

*Stuarts in the Western Desert. First regiment of the 8th Army equipped with U.S. tanks were the 8th King's Royal Irish Hussars of 4th Armoured Brigade, seen here in September 1941 with their new mounts.*

*A Stuart tank of 7th Armoured Division patrols the Qattara Depression at the time of first Alamein, July 1942.*

*M5A1 light tanks of a U.S. armored division move through the French village of St Amand to cross the Belgian border, September 1944. Leading vehicle is fitted with "prongs" – the Cullin Hedgerow Device – more usualy fitted to medium tanks to cut through hedges and foliage in close country.*

connecting rod. The bogie frames were slotted to reduce weight.

In all 1,900 M22s were ordered and deliveries began in April 1943. By February 1944 a total of 830 had been produced and at that stage further production was cancelled. A number of M22s were sent to Britain where the tank was dubbed the Locust and was used by the British in small numbers with their own airborne light tank, the Tetrarch, in the Rhine crossing operation on 24 March, 1945.

The M22 had a number of limitations. With armor only one inch thick at maximum it could be penetrated by even .50 inch armor-piercing ammunition. Its main armament of a 37mm gun had little tactical value by 1944. Its 162hp Lycoming aircooled boxer type engine was underpowered, and its mechanical reliability was

poor. After the war some Locusts ended up, via Belgian scrap dealers, with the Egyptian army.

## U.S. Armored Formations

During the course of World War II the U.S. armored division — as was also the case with the British and German armored divisions — was reorganized several times in the light of tactical, logistical, and other experience. There were five reorganizations, but only two were of major importance. The first was in March 1942.

The original armored division had, on paper at least, a plethora of tanks — an armored brigade consisting of three armored regiments (two light and one medium) and a field artillery regiment of two battalions. Each of the armored regiments had three battalions. In the new

*M4A1 light tanks of the Red Army fording a river in the Taman Peninsula, Eastern Front, in 1943. Soviets received these vehicles under Lease-Lend.*

*Stuart of the 8th Hussars camouflaged with a 'sun shield' to make it look like a truck on the approach march to Sidi Rezegh, November 19 1941.*

organization the armored brigade set-up disappeared and along with it one of the armored regiments, leaving instead two Combat Commands, popularly known as CCA and CCB, and two armored regiments. Each of these had three tank battalions but the proportion of light and medium tanks was changed, there now being two medium battalions to one light battalion in each regiment.

The artillery in the division was also re-organized. There were now three identical artillery regiments under a divisional artillery commander instead of two battalions in an artillery regiment in the armored brigade and one battalion in the division's support element. For reconnaissance there was an armored reconnaissance battalion and an attached air observation squadron. The support element had an armored infantry regiment and an engineer battalion. The services were a signals company, a maintenance company, a quartermaster truck battalion, and a medical battalion.

The second major change took place in September

*M4A1 Light tank of 17th Cavalry under camouflage in Germany early in 1945. Fitted in front is a Culin hedgerow device, a brilliant invention devised in the field in Normandy.*

*M3 Light tank of 2/6th Australian Armoured Regiment in the fighting on the Buna track in Papua, December 1942, when the tanks showed their value in bunker-busting.*

1943. The first major re-organization had resulted in what were called "heavy" divisions. This one turned the armored divisions into "light" divisions. The main difference was a further reduction in the division's tank strength by replacing the two armored regiments (a total of six tank battalions) with three tank battalions. This did not mean however that the number of tanks was halved. Within each new tank battalion there was an increase from three tank companies to four, and instead of there being light battalions and medium battalions there was now only a single type of tank battalion, three of its companies equipped with medium tanks, and one with light tanks. In addition each tank battalion had a headquarters company and a service company. The tank strength was now 263 — about one third less than under the "heavy" table.

Other changes in the "light" armored division included the addition of a third combat command which controlled the division's reserve on the march and hence was known as the reserve command, CCR or sometimes CCC. The armored reconnaissance battalion was changed to a cavalry reconnaissance squadron, taking in the reconnaissance companies from the armored regiments as its troops.

As well as the 16 armored divisions, all of which fought against the European Axis powers either in North Africa, Italy or North-West Europe, the United States also raised (at the peak in 1944) 65 separate tank battalions. One third of these fought in the Pacific theater, the other two thirds in Europe (including North Africa). Only one battalion, the 750th, fought in both Europe and the Pacific. In addition to these 65, there were another 29 in course of organization, and there were 17 amphibian tractor battalions all but one of which fought in the Pacific theater.

After the 1943 re-organization had made a single

type of tank battalion in the armored divisions the separate tank battalions were also re-organized on the same basis so that the non-divisional battalion became interchangeable with the tank battalion of an armored division, thus simplifying training, supply, reinforcement, and administration.

There were also nearly 200 mechanized cavalry units, 73 of them non-divisional, the rest attached to divisions. Each infantry division had its cavalry reconnaissance troop. Each armored division also had its divisional cavalry unit called an "armored reconnaissance battallion" under the heavy set-up and a "cavalry reconnaissance squadron, mechanized" under the light. The U.S. Marine Corps also had its divisional tank battalions.

## Japanese Tank Development

Japanese enthusiasm for tanks began in 1925 when a development program was initiated and a tank unit formed. In order to equip the new tank unit, until Japan had built her own, ordnance officers were sent to Europe and the United States to buy tanks. Because there were insufficient Vickers Mediums for Britain's own tank force the British War Office refused to authorize the sale of any of these. In France, there were plenty of obsolete Renault FTs available, but the Japanese had already evaluated these and only purchased a few for training purposes. In the United States J. Walter Christie was anxious to sell his new idea for a tank, but it was only an idea and what the Japanese wanted were actual tanks.

Thus the Japanese were forced to rely entirely on their own tank production, despite qualms on the part of the High Command because of the embryonic state of the Japanese automotive industry, on which the tank production basically would depend. The plan was to

*Three-quarter left rear view of Type 89 'B' Medium tank with ditching tail. Fuel tanks are over the tracks.*

*an M4A1 of 43rd Tank Battalion, 12th Armored Div. XXI Corps, 7th Army, accompanies half-tracks (background) into the town of Neustadt, Germany, which has just been surrendered to U.S. forces, April 16, 1945.*

*Type 89 'B' Medium tank of the Imperial Naval Landing Force in Shanghai.*

*Type 89 Medium tank with single sloping front plate and 'saucepan' cupola. This model has sometimes been referred to as Type 92 Medium tank.*

build a light tank weighing under 10 tons and similar to the Renault FT, and a so-called heavy tank under 20 tons and similar to the British Medium. Because of the urgency with which the Japanese now regarded the need for their own tanks the time between starting design work and completing the prototype in February 1927 was only 21 months. Later, with modifications, Prototype No 1 became the Type 95 Heavy tank, the characteristics of which were:

| | |
|---|---|
| Weight | 25.6 tons |
| Length | 21′ 3″ |
| Width | 8′ 11″ |
| Height | 9′ 6″ |
| Main gun turret armament | Type 94 70mm Tank Gun and one machine-gun |
| Forward gun turret | Type 94 37mm Gun |
| Rear machine gun turret | One machine-gun |
| Armor thickness | 30mm |
| Engine output | 290hp |
| Crew | 5 |

A month after Prototype No 1 had been completed the Japanese took delivery of a prototype Vickers Model C tank which had not been adopted for the British Army for whom it had been developed. While the tank was doing a steep climb during its preliminary trial runs fumes from carburettor overflow seeped inside and were ignited by an engine backfire. The engine was burnt out and the two Vickers engineers who were in the tank were badly scalded. A replacement engine arrived six months later. The importance of this accident was that it later spurred the Japanese to develop diesel engines for tanks because it highlighted the desirability of using fuel with a high flashpoint under combat conditions. Furthermore, since Japan had to import all its oil it was more advantageous to use diesel engines which have a higher thermal efficiency and smaller fuel consumption than gasoline ones, and there is less loss through evaporation. Japanese tank diesel engine development resulted in a prototype in 1933 which was tested during the following year and officially adopted in 1936. The Japanese were thus the first to produce a tank diesel engine, although the Russians would dispute this claim.

## Type 89 Medium

Tests with Prototype No 1 made the Japanese reevaluate the performance capabilities that were required from a tank which was to be used for the direct support of infantry. This second home-produced tank, Prototype No 2, was completed in April 1929 and after thorough testing was standardized first as the Type 89 Light tank and then later, when the Type 95 Light tank appeared, as the Type 89 Medium tank. The characteristics of the standardized tank were:

| | |
|---|---|
| Weight | 9.6 tons (later as a result of a number of modifications asked for in the field the final weight was 11.3 tons) |
| Length overall | 14′ 2″ (later a tail was added to improve trench crossing which made the length 18′ 11″) |

*Column of Type 89 Medium tanks with infantry moving forward after an attack.*

*Three-quarter left front view of Type 3 Medium tank (Chi-Nu).*

*Type 97 Medium tanks with radio antennae round turret tops. The cupola hatch was of a most unusual design. It had two flaps, one shaped like a crab's claw which fitted round the other when the hatch was closed.*

| | |
|---|---|
| Width | 7′ |
| Height | 7′ 2″ |
| Armor thickness | all important areas 17mm |
| Maximum speed | 17mph |
| Armament | 57mm gun in turret, machine-gun offset in rear of turret and bow machine gun |
| Crew | 4 |

When diesel engines were introduced Type 89 Mediums with a gasoline engine were designated Type 89 A and those with diesel engines Type 89 B. A number of other modifications were made to the Type 89 during the course of its career. Originally it had a short front plate with a door on the right, a vertical front plate above this with a bow machine-gun on the right and the driver's visor on the left, a small "saucepan" cupola hinged to the top of the turret, and five small return rollers mounted along a girder. All these characteristics were subsequently modified. The two front plates were combined into one long sloping front, the turret was re-designed with a flattish cupola that had a split lid opening in two halves, the positions of the bow· machine-gun and the driver were interchanged so that the driver was on the right and the bow machine-gun on the left, the girder was removed and the return rollers reduced to four, the skirting was re-designed, and a ditching tail was added to improve the tank's trench crossing performance. Type 89 Mediums which had been partially or wholly modified as described above have sometimes been referred to by other designations viz. Type 92 Medium and Type 94 Medium tanks.

Meanwhile in 1930 the Japanese bought several Renault NC tanks. These were armed with a 37mm gun or a machine-gun, had a speed of 11mph weighed 7.9 tions, and had a crew of two. With their own Type 89 already in production the Japanese had no real need of these tanks, but during the earlier visit of the Japanese Purchasing Mission to France they had mentioned the performance requirements they had in mind. Renault had developed a tank to meet these requirements without any commitment on the Japanese part. Now that they were built however they felt it only courteous to buy them. It was a poor purchase. The tanks were used, together with the Type 89 Mediums, during the first Shanghai Incident in 1932. They were little better than the Renault FTs and acquired a bad reputation among their crews for engine over-heating and suspension weaknesses.

## Type 92 Heavy Combar Car

As in other countries at this period mechanization and motorization of the cavalry began. Experiments were carried out with armored cars and in 1930 an amphibious half-track was developed for cavalry use but was not adopted. Two years later the Type 92 Heavy Combat Car was produced for standard cavalry use. Although designated a combat car it was in fact a light tank, the designation being obligatory, as in France and the United States, because the vehicle was used by the cavalry which was not allowed to have tanks as part of its equipment.

The Type 92 Heavy Combat Car weighed 3.4 tons. It had a three-man crew and was powered by a 6-cylinder air-cooled gasoline engine of 45mph which gave it a top road speed of 25mph. It was armed with a 12.7mm machine-gun beside the driver and a 6.5mm machine-gun in an all-round traverse turret. Armor was 6mm, length 13′ 1″, width 5′ 3″, height 6′ 3″. As well as being

*Three-quarter right front view of the Type 94 Tankette with full stowage and equipment and with all its hatches open.*

109

issued to armored car units of cavalry brigades as a combat car the Type 92 was also issued to tank units as a light tank. During the Jehol Operation in Inner Mongolia in 1933 an armored car unit with Type 92s was part of the Japanese cavalry brigade involved. Some were also used for reconnaissance as part of the tank company attached to the mechanized brigade which spearheaded the attack.

## Tankettes

Like a number of other countries Japan bought several Vickers Carden-Loyd Mark VI light armored vehicles. From these was developed the Japanese Type 94 tankette which, unlike the Mark VI, had a small turret mounting a machine-gun. The most notable feature of this vehicle was the "see-saw" or bell-crank "scissors" type of suspension which was invented by Major (later Lieutenant-General) Tomio Hara and subsequently became widely used for other Japanese tanks. It was used for the first time on the Type 94.

The improved Type 94 mounted a 37mm gun as well as having adjustments made to the suspension. In 1937 these improvements were incorporated at the production stage, together with a 65hp diesel engine, and the new model was designated Type 97 tankette. Some mounted a 37mm, some a machine-gun. Weight was 4.2 tons, length 12', width 5' 11", height 5' 10". The maximum speed was 26mph. Originally produced to act as a supply, command and liaison vehicle the Types 94—97 tankettes were most frequently used as miniature tanks. In World War II, the Greater East Asia War as the Japanese call it, the tankettes were primarily used to keep open lines of communication and were originally issued on the basis of one company per infantry division. On many occasions, however, they were used as stop-gaps when deliveries of regular tanks failed.

The main tank equipping the independent tank company attached to the mechanized brigade which attacked Jehol was the Type 89. During the operation the tank revealed its Achilles heel: with a top speed of only 15mph it was unable to keep up with the motorized infantry in their 40mph trucks and the field artillery which was drawn by 25mph tractors. For a mechanized formation, of which this was the first — it was established at Kungchuling north of Mukden in 1933 — it became clear that a fast-moving light tank was necessary. Thus the Type 95 Light was designed and the Type 89 redesignated as a medium tank.°

## Type 95 Light

Mitsubishi Heavy Industries Ltd began work on the design of a new light tank in July 1933. The specification called for a vehicle weighing 7 tons, with a top speed of 25mph, a 37mm gun as a main armament in a fully traversing turret and a machine-gun in the hull adjacent to the driver. Armor was to be 12mm thick. The

*The basis on which the Japanese designated their equipment, including tanks, was the year of the Emperor's reign in which it was adopted. The reign began in the year 2586 (Western year 1926). Up to Western year 1940 the last two digits only were used. Thus the Type 89 Medium was adopted in the year 2589 (Western year 1929). From the year 2600 (Western year 1940) designations were simplified. Equipment adopted that year was called Type 100, followed by Type 1 for the year 2601, Type 2 for the year 2 602 and so on.*

*Three-quarter left front view of Type 97 Tankette, first design plan, with the driver and the engine side by side forward and the turret with its machine-gun located aft.*

*Type 94 Tankettes fording a river in China.*

power plant was to be the same as in the Type 89B with 110hp output and was to be situated in the right rear of the tank. Drive through front sprockets. Hara's "see-saw" suspension: two twin-wheeled bogies per side operating through bell-cranks and resisted by horizontally mounted helical compression springs. Crew of three: commander/gunner, driver, and machine-gunner.

The first prototype was completed in June 1934. A year later a second prototype was embarked upon and completed in November 1935 after five months work. This was standardized as the Type 95 Light tank, called the Ke-Go or more usually Ha-Go. The actual weight was 7.3 tons. Length was 14' 1", width 6' 9", height 7' 6". The Ha-Go was issued to the mechanized brigades and those units in northern Manchuria that received it found that when the tank crossed the furrows of the kaoliang fields severe pitching resulted. To overcome this the suspension was modified. The bogie arms were inverted and a small roller was added to each between the pairs of normal bogie wheels.

Later the firepower of the Type 95 was increased by mounting a new 37mm gun which had a muzzle velocity of 2,215 feet per second instead of 1,886. Also a machine-gun was added in the rear of the turret facing outwards at five o'clock. This addition showed clearly the tank's conception as an infantry support weapon. The Type 95 was the most widely used of all Japanese tanks in World War II.

An amphibious tank Type 2, Ka-Mi, weighing 12.3 tons was developed from the Type 95 Ha-Go for use by the Japanese Navy. This was followed by a heavier Type 3, Ka-Chi, and in 1945 by a Type 5 To-Ku.

## Type 97 Medium

In 1935, although the Type 89s were still popular with their crews the state of the art in Great Britain suggested that a faster more powerful tank was needed to meet the requirements of a main battle tank in mobile opera-

tions. Two prototypes were built to a given specification, one by Mitsubishi, the other by the Osaka Army Arsenal. Both were to be armed with the 57mm gun. Mitsubishi's Chi-Ha had a speed of 24mph, weighed 13.3 tons, and as well as the 57mm main armament had two machine-guns. The Chi-Ha was 18' 2" long, 7' 8" wide, 7' 4" high, had a crew of four, and was powered by a 170hp air-cooled diesel engine. Armor was 25mm. The Osaka Chi-Ni was lighter and slower. Speed was 19mph and weight 9.6 tons. The engine was a 135hp diesel unit. There was only one machine-gun in addition to the main armament. The crew was only three — a tactical disadvantage in that the commander was also the gunner. The Chi-Ni also had 25mm armor. In order to allow for future up-gunning the diameter of the turret ring in both tanks was made as large as possible. This turned out to be a wise provision.

The Chi-Ni was the cheaper of the two and this made it the favorite for adoption until on 7 July 1937 the

*Three-quarter right front view of Type 97 Tankette, second design plan, with the engine at the rear. This version has a gun mounted in the turret instead of a machine-gun.*

探照燈
砲塔蓋
砲塔
砲眼
銃眼
車体
前部出入口扉
牽環
履帯
起動輪
下部転輪
ばね覆
揺臂
上部転輪
誘導輪

*Three-quarter right rear view of Type 95 Light tank prototype completed by Mitsubishi Heavy Industries Ltd in June 1934.*

*Three quarter left front view. The prototype had straight hull sides but the production vehicles had the fighting compartment widened to overhang the tracks and thus increase space inside.*

拳銃口
展望窓
消音器
後部出入口扉
後部牽環

China Incident (as the Japanese called it) broke out. Economy at once became less important than power and the Chi-Ha was selected. A number of improvements were made before the tank was standardized as the Type 97 Medium. Weight had gone up to 14.8 tons. Radio was installed. The suspension was the bell-crank system with helical springs but no shock absorbers. There were six double rubber tired wheels each side. Mounted in pairs the four center wheels operated against horizontally mounted compression spring while the front and rear wheels acted on slopingly mounted compression springs.

When three armored divisions were organized in 1942 the Type 97 Medium, when available, was what would now be called the main battle tank of those divisions.

## Up-Gunning of Medium Tanks

The first major change was to mount a new turret on the Chi-Ha to allow it to carry a long-barrelled Type 1 47mm gun instead of the 57mm gun. The two machine-guns were retained. Combat weight was increased by about 1,000 lbs. The tank was described as the Type 97 Medium-Modified or the new turret Chi-Ha.

Next came the Type 1 Medium of 1940, the Chi-He. This was the Type 97 Medium with a Type 1 47mm gun and other modifications including a Type 100 diesel engine with horsepower increased from 170 to 230. Armor in some areas was increased to 50mm. The welded structure was another feature. The Chi-He had two machine-guns. Weight 16.9 tons.

The Chi-He was followed by the Chi-Nu, Type 3 Medium, which was armed with a long-barrelled 75mm gun of the Type 90 field artillery class. Weight 18.7 tons. Because of limited factory capacity only small numbers of the Chi-He and Chi-Nu were built. Indeed Japan built only 3,600 tanks and 900 self-propelled guns during World War II. The most powerful of these tanks was the next in succession after the Chi-Nu. This was the Type 4 Medium, the Chi-To. It was armed with a 75mm gun of the anti-aircraft class and two machine-guns. Weight 29.5 tons. The Chi-To was kept in Japan

for the defense of the homeland. A Type 5 Medium, the Chi-ri, with a 37mm gun as well as a 75mm and two machine-guns was at the prototype stage when the war ended.

## Light Tank Development

A successor to the Type 95 Light tank was designed in 1938, but as the Army High Command was satisfied with the performance of the Type 95, as were its users, this successor was not produced until 1942 when it appeared as the Type 98 Light — a delay which caused chagrin among the tank's designers, who included General Hara. It was a three-man tank, slightly lower, shorter, lighter and faster than the Type 95 and was known as the Ke-Ni. Suspension was of the standard see-saw type but with six wheels in three pairs each side for better stability. Main armament was a Type 100 37mm gun with a muzzle velocity of 2,493 feet/sec, and there was a coaxial 7.7mm machine-gun. The engine was a Type 100 6-cylinder air-cooled diesel of 130hp giving a maximum speed of 32mph. Range was 190 miles.

The Type 2 Light (Ke-To) was a Type 98 with a cylindrical turret mounting a higher velocity 37mm gun. Types 3 and 4 Light tanks (Ke-Ri and Ke-Nu) were both modified Type 95, the Type 3 with a 57mm gun, the Type 4 with the original Type 97 turret which increased the tank's weight to 8.3 tons. A prototype Type 5 (Ke-Ho) was also produced which was to mount a 47mm gun.

In his *Profile* of Japanese Medium tanks General Hara pointed out that in the Japanese army armored tactics always lagged behind engineering achievements. "There is no denying that Japanese military doctrine initially lacked enthusiasm in the tactical application of armor. On the China battlefields the Japanese army became accustomed to fighting badly equipped Chinese forces and could not rid itself of the direct infantry support concept which could have been handled more efficiently with many tankette type armored vehicles. Under the circumstances it can be said that Japan completely lacked tactical and material preparations in armored warfare. When the shortcomings were realized and a belated changeover was attempted it was too late."

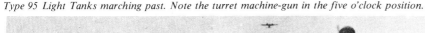

*Type 95 Light Tanks marching past. Note the turret machine-gun in the five o'clock position.*

*Three-quarter right front view of Type 97 Medium tank – Modified.*

*Three-quarter left front view of Type 4 Medium tank, Chi-To, the most powerful Japanese tank.*

*Russian IS-3s in the Victory Parade in Berlin, September 1945. The lifting flap to allow full elevation of the 122mm gun can be seen on the nearest tank.*

# VI
# 1944—45: The Last Year

The last year of the war saw a number of new tanks in action for the first time. The Germans introduced the Royal Tiger in May 1944, the British had the Cromwell and the Comet and, at the very end, the Centurion. The Americans brought on a new medium, the Pershing, and a new light tank, the Chaffee. In Japan, as we have seen, up-gunning of both medium and light tanks continued. Russia was developing its T-34 into the T-44 which proved to be only a stepping-stone to the much longer-lived T-54. In the last few months the IS-3 appeared, causing a sudden concern among the Western allies when they saw it for the first time at the Victory Parade in Berlin in September 1945. The main change in the IS-3 was its armor arrangement. While performance and main armament were the same as for its predecessor the re-designed turret and hull, influenced by the T-34, made it the most advanced heavy tank of its time. So menacing did it seem that it led to a number of hurried, and not always successful attempts by the British, Americans and French to counter what was called the heavy gun threat. The British produced the Conqueror, the Americans the M103. France, which had been liberated in 1944, returned to tank design with the ARL44 and the AMX50, although neither was ready in time to equip the three French armored divisions that took part in the defeat of Germany in the West. Sher-

mans and Stuarts equipped the *divisions blindées* just as they equipped the American armored divisions and tank battalions and so many of the British and Commonwealth armored regiments.

## Last British Cruisers
The British cruisers Marks I to VI were all tanks that had started their design life pre-war. The later cruisers were war-time designs. In 1941 a specification was laid down for a cruiser with front armor of 75/65mm, weighing 24 tons, and mounting a 6-pounder (57mm) gun on a 60 inch turret ring. The tanks that resulted from this were the A24 Cruiser Mark VII Cavalier (weight 27 tons) and the A27 Cruiser Mark VIII (27.5 tons). Fitted with a Liberty engine the A27(L) was called the Centaur, with a Meteor engine the A27(M) was the Cromwell. Cavaliers, of which 500 were built, were not used in action as gun tanks but about half were converted to armored OPs for artillery regiments of armored divisions in North-West Europe 1944—45. Cromwells, on the other hand, equipped the 22nd Armoured Brigade of the British 7th Armoured Division as well as five armored reconnaissance regiments of armored divisions in 21 Army Group.

There were four marks of Centaur and eight marks of Cromwell Centaurs I and II had a 6-pounder as the

*Russian T-44, a test-bed for later main battle tanks.*

main armament, Centaur III had a 75mm, Centaur IV, which was a support tank, had a 95mm gun. Cromwells I, II and III were 6-pounder armed, IV, V and VII had a 75mm, and VI and VIII had a 95mm for close support. Cromwells VII and VIII had the armor increased, mainly on the front, to 101mm. The first production Centaurs were delivered at the end of 1942, the first Cromwells in 1943. There were a number of Centaur and Cromwell special purpose tanks — OP, anti-aircraft, bulldozer, ARV.

Lengthened Cromwell chassis were used in 1943—44 for the production of 200 Challengers (A30) mounting a 17 pounder. The Challenger had the role of a tank destroyer in support of the other cruisers, a troop typically consisting of three Cromwells and one Challenger. An alternative version of the A30 was developed as a self-propelled anti-tank gun; it was called Avenger. The order for 230 Avengers was not fulfilled until

1946 because by the time the pilot model was ready in 1944 the American M10 had been adopted for service in British tank destroyer regiments. The M10 mounted a 3 inch gun on a M4A2 or M4A3 chassis.

The next tank in the cruiser line was the Comet, a development of the Cromwell designed to overcome the weaknesses of the Challenger which were attributable mainly to mounting a big gun on a comparatively small hull. Developed under the ordnance specification A34 the first production Comets were delivered in September 1944 and sent to Belgium in November. The armored units of the British 11th Armoured Division, including the divisional armored reconnaissance regiment, were the only ones to be re-equipped with Comets before the fighting in Europe was over. Their re-equipment, begun in December, was interrupted by the Ardennes offensive and completed in March. The Comet weighed 32.7 tons with maximum armor of

*Cromwell of 8th King's Royal Irish Hussars, 7th British Armoured Division landing in Normandy on D+1, 7 June 1944.*

*The Challenger with lengthened Cromwell chassis and mounting a 17 pounder was a tank destroyer in support of other cruisers.*

*Three-quarter left rear view of the Type 97 Medium Tank – Modified.*

117

*Cromwell of 15th/19th The King's Royal Hussars, 11th British Armoured Divsion in the ruins of Udem, 28 February 1945.*

101mm. Its main armament was a 77mm gun which was, in fact, a slightly less powerful version of the 17 pounder (76.2mm) with a caliber of 75mm but which was re-named in order to avoid confusion with other British and American guns in service. The Comet remained in service with the British Regular army until 1959.

## Centurion

The Comet was really the last of the cruiser tanks. Although the Centurion which succeeded it (and to which it contributed in development) was designed as a cruiser, by the time it came into production in 1945 the idea of a multi-purpose "capital" tank had taken the place of the previous two-type concept — cruisers and "I" tanks. The Centurion, developed under the ordnance designation A41, was regarded as meeting the "capital" tank requirement and thus became the first of what are now called main battle tanks. Although six Centurions were rushed to the 22nd Armoured Brigade

*T-34/85 in Wenceslaus Square, Prague, 1945.*

of the British 7th Armoured Division in May 1945 they arrived too late for testing in combat and the Centurion had to wait for the Korean War to prove its worth. That it did so is evidenced by the fact that the Centurion was still in service in some armies thirty-five years after it was first produced.

## Koenigstiger or Royal Tiger

The last German tank to go into service in World War II was the Tiger Ausf B or Koenigstiger, known to its enemies in the West as the Tiger II, King Tiger or Royal Tiger. It was put into production in December 1943 and first saw action in May 1944 on the Russian front. In August it came into the battle in Normandy. It was a huge tank, the heaviest ever to appear on any battlefield. Its battle weight was nearly 69 tons, it was 33' 8" long (including gun overhang), 12' 4" wide (with wide tracks; with narrow tracks it was 10' 9"), and it was just over 10' high. Its main armament was a 21' long 8.8cm KWK43 L/71. It also had three 7.92mm machine-guns, one mounted coaxially, one mounted in the hull front, and the third mounted on the cupola for AA defence. It was designed and built so that it would be capable of dealing with any new tank the Russians could possibly produce.

In August 1942 both Porsche and Henschel were asked to submit designs for the tank which was to have thicker armor than the Tiger Ausf E, with sloped plates as on the Panther and the Russian T-34. Porsche redesigned his Tiger (P) to conform to the specification. His design was rejected, as was his second attempt, although the construction of turrets for the latter was begun and these turrets were later used on some of the production Tiger IIs. Henschel's first design was also rejected but the second one was accepted and a prototype was delivered in October 1943.

In all 484 Tiger Ausf Bs were produced. The first 50 had Porsche turrets, the remainder had a modified

Comets seen here crossing the Weser on 7 April 1945 were the last of the cruiser series.

A battalion of Royal or King Tigers (Koenigstiger, Tiger Ausf. B, also known as Tiger II) drawn up for inspection.

*US infantry cautiously approach a burning Panther which has just been savaged by a rocket attack from fighters, Normandy, June 1944.*

*Early production Tiger Ausf. B with the Porsche turret which was distinguished by the bulged commander's cupola on the left side.*

turret specially designed for the Ausf B with thicker armor and eliminating the re-entrant angle under the trunnion axis. The gun barrel was also changed from monobloc to two piece construction. Some of these new barrels were also retro-fitted to the Porsche turret.

The Royal Tiger was a logical development of the Tiger I, incorporating all the good points of the Panther and armed with the largest caliber and caliber length gun to be used operationally by the Germans in a tank mounting during the war. Internally the vehicle followed the usual German layout with the engine at the rear, the driver and bow gunner in the hull and the Commander, gunner, and loader in the turret. Radio equipment was located above the gearbox to the left of the hull machine-gunner. The armor, particularly that on the front of the tank, was the thickest ever used on a tank that was to be produced on a large scale. The front glacis was 150mm set at 40 degrees; the nose plate was 100mm set at 55 degrees.

The engine was a Maybach HL230 P30 of 600hp giving a top road speed of 25.7mph and a range of 100 miles. Cross-country speed and range were 9—12mph and 75 miles respectively. The suspension had torsion

bars as the springing medium, the general assembly being similar to that used by the Tiger I except that overlapping bogie wheels were used instead of the overlapped and interleaved system of the Panther and Tiger I. This helped to get rid of the problem of the tracks jamming in shingle or freezing solid with packed snow. The track was 2′ 7″ wide and a narrower track of 2′ 2″ was used for transporting the tank on a rail flat. A limited traverse tank destroyer version of the Royal Tiger was produced. This was the Jagdtiger. It was the heaviest armored fighting vehicle to go into service in World War II. It weighed 70.5 tons, had a crew of six and was armed with the most powerful anti-tank gun to be used in the war, the 12.8cm Pak 80L/55. The front plate of the turret was 250mm thick and sloped back at 15 degrees.

## M24 Light — Chaffee

While the M5 Light tank was still based essentially on pre-war ideas the M24 Light was a tank of a new generation. It saw only limited service in World War II, its major combat career coming in Korea in 1950 when it had to face the Russian T-34/85s of North Korea.

Nonetheless it was well represented in the last six months of the fighting in Europe and in the Pacific. The M24 was named Chaffee in honor of General Adna R. Chaffee, the father of the US armored forces in the inter-war period.

The M24 was built in accordance with the common chassis concept which meant that three basic assemblies were used for the tank and for its companion vehicles — the M19 Gun Motor Carriage, the M41 Howitzer Motor Carriage and the M37 Howitzer Motor Carriage. These three basic assemblies were: first, the power pack assembly of engines, transmissions, transfer cases, fuel tanks and radiators. The engines were the standard commercial engines used in Cadillac automobiles which had proved themselves in the M5A1. This was also the case with the hydramatic transmission.

The second basic assembly was the power train, consisting of the Cletrac controlled differential permitting continuous drive to both front sprockets at all times, together with the final drive and the steering control which was provided by brake bands operating in oil. This type of steering had been in use on US tanks since its first installation in the T1E6 Light tank in the early 1930s, and it had been used in French tanks prior to that.

The third basic assembly was made up of the track, rubber-tired bogie wheels, torsion bar suspension and support rollers.

The M24 was built in Detroit by Cadillac and in Milwaukee by Massey-Harris. In order to include the companion vehicles the original order was increased to 5,000. Of these 4,731 were built: 4,070 M24s, 285 M19 GMCs, 60 M41 HMCs and 316 M37 HMCs. The first production vehicle appeared in April 1944.

*White painted for snow camouflage this newly delivered M-24 was photographed during the advance into Germany, February 1945. Tracks and road wheels are still in mint factory condition.*

The M24 Light tank had the engines (two Cadillac Model 44 T24 gasoline) and the transmission in the rear, the armament in the center and the final drive at the bow, with the engine compartment separated from the fighting compartment by a bulkhead. The driver sat at the left front with the assistant driver/radio operator on his right. Dual controls were provided. The commander was on the left of the turret with the gunner and the loader to his right. Originally only four men were intended as the crew, the assistant driver moving up to become the loader in combat.

*Pilot model of T.24 light tank 1943.*

*Reconnaissance squadron of newly arrived M-24 tanks in leaguer near Kornelmunster during the advance into Germany. Boxing Day 1944.*

The power train was adapted from that of the M5A1. It had a two speed and reverse manual shift transfer case in place of the automatic unit. For suspension the torsion bar arrangement from the M18 Tank Destroyer which was being built by another divison of General Motors was used. This type of suspension provided better riding qualities, better flotation and in turn a more stable gun platform. The turret ring was that of the M5A1 but the turret itself was larger. There was no turret basket but the crew seats rotated in the turret. The guns, a 75mm with a coaxial .30 inch Browning, and a .30 Browning in the right glacis and a .50 Browning pintle-mounted on the turret, could be fired either manually or electrically and there was hydraulically operated stabilisation in elevation. One radio was located in front of the assistant driver and one or more (if it was a command vehicle) in the rear of the turret. Armor was of welded homogeneous plate one inch thick which, being ballistically shaped, represented a $2\frac{1}{2}$ inch hull basis and a $1\frac{1}{4}$ inch turret basis. Thus the M24 was heavier and thicker armored than the M5A1 and there was more room in the turret to serve the better armament.

## M26 Medium — Pershing

Planning for a successor to the American M4 Medium, the Sherman, began as soon as the up-gunned Panzer III and Panzer IV were encountered on the Libyan battlefields in 1942. But not until February 1945 did that successor arrive with the combat troops. It eventually resulted from developments of the Medium tank T20 series, which included the T20, T22, T23, T25, and T26. Its non-appearance until the last months of the war was caused by the opposing views of a tank's purpose held by different influential departments of the US army. Army Ground Forces' doctrine was that the proper role of a tank was as a maneuvering element and that it should not engage in tank-versus-tank battles. The task of destroying enemy tanks should be left to the artillery and the tank destroyers. By early 1943 the Tank Destroyer force had 106 active battalions (its maximum), almost as many as the total number of tank battalions. Both Ordnance and the Armored Force disagreed with this doctrine. They held that the best anti-tank weapon was another tank. They wanted a tank with a 90mm gun to take on the new Panthers and Tigers.

However, there was a point of disagreement between Ordnance and the Armored Force. The former wanted to mount the 90mm gun on a new tank; the latter believed that a new tank chassis would not be fully developed in time to be of use in the war and wanted to modify the Sherman in order to mount the heavier gun. Army Ground Forces had no objection to a new tank. It was the heavier gun that worried them. A heavier gun might encourage the tanks carrying it to take on other tanks. Between the three points of view there was no compromise and all requests for production of a new tank carrying a heavier gun were refused.

The Gordian knot was cut by experience on the battlefield in Italy where the Panthers and Tigers were ignoring doctrine and destroying Shermans. Shortly before the landings in Normandy the US command in Europe requested that all production of 75mm and 76mm medium tanks be stopped. What was wanted in future was the 90mm gun and the 105mm howitzer as tank armament.

From the various T20 series developments there were two which would meet the requirements — the T25 and the T26. The T25 provided the better balance between firepower, mobility, and armor with the 500hp Ford GAF engine that was available for both. But the T26 had thicker armor, 2 to 4 inches (50.8mm to 101.6mm) thick compared with the T25's 1½ to 3½ inches, and the experience of the troops in Normandy made them more interested in protection than mobility. The T26 was chosen and standardized in March 1945, first as a heavy tank and then as the Medium M26 Pershing. It weighed 41.1 tons, had a crew of five, and as well as its 90mm main armament had a coaxial .30 Browning

machine-gun, another .30 Browning in the right front of the hull, and a .50 Browning pintle-mounted on the turret. Suspension was torsion bars with six rubber tired bogie wheels and five return rollers each side. It was 20′9″ long, 11′6″ wide, and 9′1″ high. It had a maximum speed of 30mph and a range of 110 miles. miles.

The first 20 Pershings to go on active service reached Antwerp, Belgium early in February 1945. They were divided between the 3rd and 9th Armored Divisions of First US Army. The next shipment was allotted to 2nd and 5th Armored Divisions of Ninth US Army, and 11th Armored Division of Third US Army. It was 3rd Armored Division that introduced the Pershing into action with an attack across the Roer River on 26 February. Ten days later the Pershing platoon of 14th Tank Battalion of 9th Armored Division under Lieutenant Grimball took part in one of the most significant actions of the war when, with Company A of the 27th Armored Infantry under Lieutenant Timmerman, they captured intact the Remagen bridge across the Rhine and opened the way into the German heartland.

The Pershing's main combat career came in Korea where, with Sherman "Easy Eights", it came to the relief of the hard-pressed Chaffees.

*Pershing tank of 9th Infantry Regiment, 2nd Infantry Division, in defense position at the Maktong River in Korea, September 1950.*